SAY IT WITH PRESENTATIONS

HOW TO DESIGN AND DELIVER SUCCESSFUL BUSINESS PRESENTATIONS

GENE ZELAZNY

McGraw-Hill

New York   San Francisco   Washington, D.C.   Auckland   Bogotá   Caracas   Lisbon   London   Madrid
Mexico City   Milan   Montreal   New Delhi   San Juan   Singapore   Sydney   Tokyo   Toronto

Library of Congress Cataloging-in-Publication Data
Zelazny, Gene.
    Say it with presentations : how to design and deliver
successful business presentations / by Gene Zelazny.
        p.   cm.
    ISBN 0-07-135407-7
    1. Business presentations—Graphic methods.   I. Title.
HF5718.22.Z453   1999
    668.4'5—dc21   99-41282
                                                         CIP

McGraw-Hill

A Division of The McGraw·Hill Companies

    2 3 4 5 6 7 8 9 0 DOC/DOC   0 4 3 2 1 0

ISBN 0-07-135407-7

*The sponsoring editor for this book was Jeffrey Krames; the editing supervisor
was John Morriss, and the production supervisor was Tina Cameron. This book
was set in Palatino by North Market Street Graphics.*

Printed and bound by R. R. Donnelley & Sons Company.

This book is printed on recycled, acid-free paper containing a
minimum of 50% recycled, de-inked fiber.

*To **Marvin Bower** for creating the playground
known as McKinsey & Company
and
to the thousands of friends and colleagues in the Firm
who gave me the space to play in it*

*Here it is almost 40 years later and
I'm still running around with sand in my sneakers.*

ACKNOWLEDGMENTS

Recently I heard the expression, **"the gift of feedback."** It meant a lot to me, especially when I thought of the professionals who supported me in creating this book. Thank you all, for being such an important part of this book, and of my life.

Sara Roche for your uncompromising standards of quality in editing the ideas, the structure, the words. Sara recently retired from McKinsey & Company, where she made friends of all those who had the privilege of working with her for 32 years. Sara also edited my first book, *Say It with Charts.*

Vera Deutsch for making me look good. She's the talented graphics designer who added her magic touch to the look and feel of the book, as she did with *Say It with Charts.*

Dan Nevins for your gift of humor with the illustrations.

Zac Enco for giving your dad, **Bill Enco,** the time he needed to help shape the chapter on selecting media in the next decade.

Ellen Lesser for your patient, sensitive, constructive advice when I needed it most.

Judy Marcus for sharing your professional insights, for bringing out my softer, gentler voice, and for holding my hand as we move through life together.

CONTENTS

INTRODUCTION

SO YOU'VE BEEN ASKED TO GIVE A PRESENTATION

So you've been asked to give a business presentation. I stress *you've been asked* because, for most of us, there's no way we would ever volunteer.

"Don't tell *me* to give the presentation," the little voice in your head shouts:

> "*You* persuade the local city council that we should place the toxic waste dump in their backyard."

> "*You* advise the company founder to shut down operations in two plants and put 2000 employees out of work."

> "*You* tell the business unit leaders why they need to cut costs in their departments by 40 percent."

> "*You* convince the board of directors to approve a 32 percent cut in wages for the 7000 employees—from chairman to cook—for the company to survive."

Would you volunteer for assignments like these? I rest my case.

So *you've been asked* to give a business presentation.

"What are you, crazy?" the voice persists. "You want me to go through what happened to Jay J.? Remember when he started his presentation with, 'Today's purpose is to . . . ,' only to hear the CEO say, 'No, that's not our purpose.'? Or when only 9 of the 75 people Sara R. invited showed up? Or when they didn't have the right cable to connect Michele Z.'s laptop to the LCD projector?"

So *you've been asked* to give a business presentation.

"And besides," the voice pleads, "I don't need the sweaty palms, the trembling knees, the butterflies in the pit of my stomach, the embarrassment of an unfortunate ad-lib, the fear of making a mistake, or worse, the anxiety that I won't be able to answer the questions."

So *you've been asked* to give a business presentation.

"And furthermore," the voice whimpers, "I don't have the time. Do you have any idea of the work that's waiting on my desk? Do you know how much time it's going to take to plan the presentation, to get the story line organized, to get the visuals and the handouts produced, to rehearse, rehearse, rehearse? Do you know how much it's going to cost?"

So *you're going to give the presentation.*

Why fight it? You knew all along you'd have to do it. That's where this book comes in. It offers insights and practical ideas derived from all the presentations I've designed and given, as well as the experiences of my friends and colleagues at McKinsey & Company for whom I've shaped presentations for more than 35 years.

I do not intend this to be a textbook from which you *learn* to design and deliver presentations. After all, you don't *learn* to ride a bicycle by reading a manual. The only way to learn is to get on the bike and fall off and get on the bike and fall off and get on the bike and ride. So it is with presentations. All this book can do is point the way; *you* have to do the pedaling.

A note of caution before getting on the bicycle. I've assumed that you've thought through the *what* of your presentation—the content—that you've thoroughly researched the supporting evidence, that the conclusions are logical, that the recommendations are realistic, and that what stands between you and success is the presentation—the vehicle that carries the facts and the ideas to your audience. There is no substitute for the confidence that comes with knowing your material. What this book is all about is the competence needed to design and deliver a presentation.

If you have only 2 minutes to spare, turn your attention to the "Audience's Bill of Rights" that follows. You may want to review it whenever you have to prepare a presentation. When you have more time, review the rest of the book to learn how to safeguard your audience's rights. Study the three chapters for how to "Define the Situation," "Design the Presentation," and "Deliver the Presentation."

Enjoy the ride.

AUDIENCE'S BILL OF RIGHTS

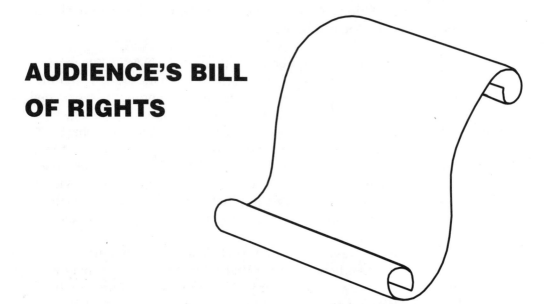

The idea of an Audience's Bill of Rights came to me from a client. At the close of one of my workshops, he said, "In this company, I am the audience. Do I have any rights?"

Here's a sampling of what I've gathered from colleagues all over the world, which may help you the next time you deliver a presentation.

ABOUT OBJECTIVES

The right to know what you want me to do or think as a result of the presentation.

The right to see the reason for my involvement.

The right to receive value for the time I devote to attending the presentation.

ABOUT RESPECT

The right to contribute to the intellectual content, and to share in the outcome.

The right to be given time to think instead of being pressed for an instant decision.

The right to be spoken neither down to nor up to, but with respect for my experience, intelligence, and knowledge.

The right to honesty when you don't have answers to my questions.

The right (that few use) to vote with my feet and walk out on poorly conceived presentations.

ABOUT TIMING

The right to know in advance how much time the presentation will take.

The right to have the presentation start and stop on time, as predetermined by my busy schedule.

The right to expect breaks once in a while, and not just for biological necessities.

ABOUT CONTENT

The right to know where we're going, how the presentation will progress.

The right to know what decisions are at issue, your rationale for your position, and the facts that support this reasoning.

The right to get the important information first. Surprise endings are for O'Henry.

ABOUT VISUALS

The right to be able to read every word on every visual without resorting to opera glasses, no matter where I sit in the audience.

The right to have complex charts explained.

ABOUT FLEXIBILITY

The right to stop for discussion, to help the group reach a shared understanding.

The right to ask questions at any time and to expect answers when I ask them, instead of being put off with, "I'll get to that later."

ABOUT DELIVERY

The right to be able to hear you from the back of the room.

The right to absorb the presentation without the distraction of wild gestures.

The right to see your face, not the back of your head, as you address the screen with the hope that the message will ricochet and hit me in the audience.

The right to enjoy your sense of humor when it helps to make a point, relieve tension, or achieve rapport.

ABOUT ENDING The right to a clear view of what has been agreed to and what will happen next.

The right to leave feeling that something meaningful was accomplished.

DEFINE THE SITUATION

The most perceptive definition of a business presentation—how it differs from, say, a lecture or a training program or a speech—comes from my friend, Sir Antony Jay. "A presentation," he says, "is an exercise in persuasion."[1] You want:

> *To persuade* the city council to place the waste dump in their backyard
>
> *To persuade* the company founder to close down the two plants
>
> *To persuade* the business unit heads to cut costs by 40 percent

And, until now, that's what you've been working on—around the clock—researching, interviewing, analyzing, and every other *-ing* that goes into surfacing the recommendations you'll want the audience to act on.

For now, do yourself a favor and push it all aside—the tomes of data, the spreadsheets, the interview notes, and

---

[1] Antony Jay and Ros Jay, *Effective Presentation* (London: Pitman Publishing, 1996).

the charts. Get a cup of your favorite brew, take a blank sheet of paper, and give yourself about 15 minutes to think about, and to record, the situation you'll be facing. Ask yourself what makes this presentation unique—different from the one you gave last week, different from the one you'll give next week. I promise you, this exercise will help you achieve the results you want from this presentation. It may even indicate that you don't need to deliver a presentation. That's fine, if you figure out a better way to do the persuading.

Here are the questions you want to answer:

> Why are you giving this presentation?
>
> Whom do you want to convince?
>
> How much time will you have for the presentation?
>
> What's the best medium to use?

Let's discuss each in more detail.

WHY ARE YOU GIVING THIS PRESENTATION?

Surely you can find better ways to spend your time than putting together a presentation. If I were to ask you to list the five things you like to do most, in order of importance, would standing in front of an audience to deliver a presentation show up? I doubt it.

Now the insight. Members of your audience HATE sitting through your presentation more than you hate giving it. No kidding. They'll do anything *not* to sit through your presentation: They'll lie, make excuses, borrow a beeper and activate it any time they feel they can't take anymore, tell their assistant to come into the room 10 minutes into the presentation and pass them a blank note so they can decide whether to stay or leave.

It's nothing personal, mind you. It's simply that they rank sitting through a presentation—anybody's presentation—one step lower than giving one. If they're like me, they rank giving presentations many, many steps lower than, for example, (1) holding hands with Judy, (2) playing tennis, (3) riding a bicycle, (4) browsing through used-book shops, or (5) having a massage.

So, please give the people at your presentation a good reason to sit through it. Make them feel indispensable to the success of your project: You need their approval for action, or you can't proceed. You must have their agreement to do something, or you can't move on. You need the benefit of their insights, of their position in the organization, of their experience with the issue, or you're stuck.

That's what defining your objective is all about. The way to a good definition is to *write, in one sentence, what, realistically, you want the members of your audience to do or to think as the result of this presentation.* There are several subtleties to this task:

> 1. *Limit it to one sentence.* If you need more than one sentence, you're not clear about your objective. Chances are your presentation will become confused among several objectives.

> 2. *Make sure that the objective is realistic.* For example, asking for an on-the-spot approval to spend millions of dollars on a new product idea may be unrealistic. The decision makers may need more than just one presentation to be persuaded.

I once worked with a couple of entrepreneurs who were putting together a presentation for an audience of interested investment bankers. I asked each of them to write down the objective of their presentation. The first wrote, "I want to impress my audience." "That's easy," I said, "send them tickets to the hottest show in town; that'll impress them." The second was more specific. He said, "I want the members of the audience to invest in my product idea." That sounded good. I offered him a single dollar bill from my wallet and asked him if he had accomplished his objective. "Of course not," he said. "What I want is $1,500,000." Yeah, sure, rub a lamp! A more realistic request would be for approval of, say, $250,000 to test market the idea, to be followed by a second presentation for approval of additional funds.

3. *Make sure that it leads to action.* The operative words are: "What do you want the audience members TO DO?"

To say that you want to review your progress to date doesn't go far enough. Would you be satisfied if, at the end of the presentation, you heard the audience say, "Thank you, we now know where you are in your work"? Chances are that you want the audience *to do* something with or about the information, or that you want approval to move ahead with the next phase of your work.

To say that you want to inform the audience or to build their understanding about something doesn't go far enough; every presentation serves to inform and to build understanding. The question is what do you want the members *to do* with the information. Be specific. For example:

> You want the local city council *to agree to sign the ordinance* that will legalize placing the waste dump in this new location.

> You want the company founder *to approve the strategy* aimed at closing the two plants.

> You want the business unit heads *to proceed with the cost reduction action program.*

A clearly defined objective has great value.

◆   *It helps to determine whether you really need to give a presentation.* You can find better things to do with your time, and none of us wants to sit through the presentation anyway. So, think hard about your objective. If you can meet it by picking up the phone, *don't* give a presentation. If you can meet it by writing a brief memo, *don't* give a presentation. Before you go forward with your presentation, be convinced that the best way to meet your objective is to have all the members of the audience hear the same message at the same time, to answer all their questions, and to give them a chance to exchange views so they can agree on what needs to be done. In short, a clearly stated objective helps you think through your communication strategy.

♦   *It helps to focus the attention and the energy of the audience.* A clearly stated objective brings focus to a presentation and thus uses the energy of the audience efficiently.

♦   *It allows you to transform your thinking* from "What do *I want* the audience to see and hear?" to "What does *the audience need* to see and hear to meet the objective?" In other words, think about your objective not in terms of what it means to you, but in terms of what it means to the audience: What do *they* need to see and hear to say Yes to what you want them to do?

♦   *Meeting your objective is the only measure of success you have for your presentation.* If you haven't stated your objective clearly, you have no way of judging if your presentation was worth the effort. If people say you're a great speaker or your visuals are gorgeous, that's nice; however, it hardly justifies the time and effort spent on a presentation.

Designing a presentation without an objective is like shaping gelatin without a mold; it can get messy and it rarely works. An objective will remind you of what you want to achieve with this particular audience at this particular time. Write one down before you decide what material to include and how to present it.

WHOM DO YOU WANT TO CONVINCE?

Here's what experienced presenters have said about knowing their audience:

> *Designing a presentation without an audience in mind is like writing a love letter and addressing it* To Whom It May Concern.
>
> Ken Haemer, AT&T

> *There is no such thing as a dumb audience. If they don't understand, it's because you can't communicate.*
>
> Harvey Golub, American Express

> *I don't analyze my audience; I analyze the* individuals *in my audience.*
>
> Lowell Bryan, McKinsey & Company

> *It's not what you say that counts; it's what they hear.*
>
> Red Auerbach, Boston Celtics

I'm sure you'll agree that you'd talk differently to a group of bankers about the effect of, for instance, technology in the banking industry than you would to a class of elementary school students. You'd talk differently to top management about improving the effectiveness of the sales force than you would to the salespeople. Therefore, one of the most important steps in defining the situation is to analyze your audience.

Analyzing the audience means more than identifying them. Of course, you want to know the names and titles of the individuals. Of course, you want to know how many people will attend. Analyzing them, on the other hand, means estimating how they will receive, understand, and accept your message; it means anticipating the reactions of the individuals to your message.

Among the questions you want to be sure to consider are these:

Who are the decision makers?

In any audience, some will know a great deal about the subject matter, others will know little; some will be directly affected by your message, others less so. If you design the presentation to meet everyone's needs, chances are that you'll be compromising, giving too much information for some, not enough for others, thereby running the risk of not meeting the needs of those whose support you need.

Think back to your objective. Who is in the best position to say Yes or No to what you want to accomplish? Who are the one, two, maybe three individuals who control the decision to invest in your new product idea, who have the authority to tell you to proceed with your action program, who manage the budget dollars? Shape the presentation to meet their needs. I'm not suggesting that you show disrespect to the other members of the audience; rather, I'm recommending that you focus your attention on what the decision makers need to see and hear to approve your objective.

How familiar are they with the material?

Never underestimate your audience's intelligence, or overestimate their knowledge of the material you're presenting. Do they know as much as you do about the situation? Can you use their language, their jargon? If not, you need to get their level of understanding where it needs to be so they can follow the presentation. At times, this may mean sending background information to the audience before the presentation. At other times, it may mean spending time during the presentation to discuss unfamiliar material.

How interested are they?

You care. After all, you've been spending days, weeks, maybe months on this project. You haven't slept all night putting this presentation together and rehearsing it. Do they care as much? If yes, that's great; you can get right to the material. If not, you need to spark their interest as quickly as possible to get their minds in the room and away from what's waiting for them on their e-mail, voice mail, mail mail, and so forth.

What's at stake? What does the audience stand to gain if they say Yes to the recommendations? What do they stand to lose?

Here's a story that makes the point. The controller of a leading newsweekly magazine told me about it. He noticed a "hockey stick" rise in miscellaneous expenses for his company in September. He checked the data for the past few years and, sure enough, the pattern repeated. The situation was important enough to bring to the attention of the chairman. Presentation! "What's causing the problem?" asked the chairman. My friend let him know: "Well, it appears that in September, all our reporters, journalists, columnists, editors, and researchers are providing their children with school supplies for the coming term."

The chairman thought about the situation and said, "Make sure we get the best quality."

Obviously, what the company stood to gain was a decrease in costs. Not so obviously, what the company stood to lose was the goodwill of the employees. The decision maker wasn't willing to trade the morale of the employees for the cost saving; what he stood to gain wasn't worth what he stood to lose.

In short, it's not only a matter of what you think should happen, based on your analysis of the facts; you must also think through the implications of your recommendation for the audience members as they try to implement it.

If what you want to convince them to do is such a good idea, why hasn't it been done before? Better yet, if what you want to convince them to do is such a good idea, why would they say NO?

We'd like to believe that rational people will make rational decisions when presented with facts. We'd really like that. The truth is that rational people often make decisions with their hearts, not necessarily their minds.

For example, take my smoking habit. For 33 years, I put cigarettes in my mouth. (When I enlisted in the air force, I figured that you weren't a "man" unless you had a tattoo, rode a horse, and smoked a Marlboro. I decided that one out of three was all right.) Over those years, I received the equivalent of many presentations to convince me to stop, each from a different perspective. All were clear, all were logical. None stopped me. For instance:

> *The financial presentation.* "Gene, do you have any idea what it's costing you to smoke one pack of cigarettes a day? I figured it out on this spreadsheet. At the end of the year, you could buy that magnificent tennis racquet you've been eyeing." *Made sense; didn't stop me.*

> *The visual presentation.* "Gene, I've made animated black-and-white visuals of the inside of your lungs that show how the tar is eating away at your lung

tissue for 3000 people to see on a 20-foot screen . . ." *Overwhelming image; didn't stop me.*

The punitive presentation. My doctor speaking: "Gene, it's very simple: you keep on smoking and you're going to die." *Scary message; didn't stop me.*

The emotional presentation. "Daddy," my daughters Michele and Donna plead, "we don't want to lose you." *Ouch!* That one got me to stop once—for about 20 minutes.

The point is that, at times, it isn't a case of convincing the audience of the good reasons for making a decision but rather of *overcoming the resistance* that people have to making changes. I've often said, "I don't mind change; it's the changing I hate." I knew how to cope with the problems created by my smoking, but I didn't know how to cope with the problems that would plague me when I stopped, such as, for instance, putting on weight. It was easier to stay with the old problem.

Okay. I hear your question: "What made me stop smoking?"

Over time, it was the sum of the arguments you made in your presentations, in your articles, in your TV and radio shows, plus the social pressures dictating where and when I could and could no longer smoke, at a time when I was psychologically ready to accept the recommendation.

It may be so in the business world, too: You can't always assume that the audience will accept what you're asking of them after one presentation. You may need to make sure that the audience is psychologically ready to accept the change your recommendations imply. If not, you may have to rethink the communication strategy. You may need to create a series of presentations to advance your case bit by bit. You may need to conduct a series of informal meetings with the decision makers to discuss the issues, to identify areas of compromise, until you're reasonably certain that the presentation will get the results you're planning for.

That's what happened with Mike. He asked me to review a presentation he was preparing for the board of directors. He came into my office and proceeded to present the most persuasive arguments for this company to centralize its organization: saves costs, improves decision making, shortens communication lines, yadda yadda yadda . . .

At the end of Mike's 15-minute soliloquy, I was convinced; it was too hard to argue with his logic. I advised him to proceed. Then I noticed that he was walking out of my office a little more quickly than he needed to; it was as though he were running away—as if he had gotten away with something.

As he got to the door, I lassoed him with one last question: "Mike, hold on a minute. If it's so obvious that this company should centralize, why haven't they done so before?" Then I dropped the bomb, "Why would they say No?"

Mike's face fell. He said, "I wish you hadn't asked me that question. The truth is that they won't do it." He explained that although the regional barons would nod in agreement in front of the CEO and the board members, they would not give up their power when they got back to their local divisions.

We talked about how Mike could deal with this attitude, and, as a result, he revisited his communication strategy. He went back to the regions and negotiated with each area manager. Only then could he present his recommendations successfully to the board the following month.

What will their attitudes be? Will they be for or against the recommendations?

It strikes me that if you wanted to be loved in business and you're one who gives presentations, you chose the wrong career field. The truth is that in these presentations, you're giving advice in the form of recommendations. As you know, there is no better way to make enemies than to give people advice. "Have a nice day," says the checkout clerk at the supermarket counter. I mutter under my breath, "Don't tell *me* what to do."

Now, it's true that your recommendations may not be popular, but that doesn't mean that the audience is the enemy, or that they will automatically be hostile. I've never been a fan of my dental hygienist, who repeatedly recommends that I brush my teeth and floss after every meal. Her advice is not what I want to hear. On the other hand, I understand the price I may have to pay if I don't take care of my teeth. I don't like her advice, but I see the merits of her recommendation and (but promise not to tell her) I do find myself flossing—occasionally.

For your presentations, your audience may not necessarily jump for joy upon hearing what you want them to do. If so, you need to structure the presentation in such a way as to build your case patiently before making the recommendations at the end of the presentation. More about that in the next chapter.

How do they absorb material?

Do they prefer numbers or charts? Are they color-blind? Do they "inhale" visuals? That is, do they capture the essence of an exhibit that breaks every rule of simplicity and legibility, in less time than it's taking you to read this paragraph?

It's difficult to anticipate all audience prejudices or personal quirks ("I don't like fancy slides." "I hate the color brown."). However, if you dig deep—checking with colleagues who have addressed this audience before, testing material with selected members of the audience before the presentation, discussing the audience with individuals who are close to the decision makers—you can anticipate how to cope with problems.

HOW MUCH TIME DO YOU HAVE FOR THE PRESENTATION?

As the audience assembles for your presentation, you can be sure of one question that is on everyone's mind: *"How long is this presentation going to be?"*

More often than not, you have no choice; someone has dictated the amount of time for the presentation. If you do have a say, keep in mind that shorter is better; if you can't get your message across in 1 hour, 2 hours won't necessarily make a difference.

Think about it this way: Films run about 90 minutes on average, TV shows about 22 minutes (without commercials); commercials get their message across in 30 seconds or less. Now I'll grant you that most of these have simple messages, and a business presentation is more complex. Still, there's a direct relationship between the length of the presentation and the degree to which the venetian blinds close over the audience's eyes.

As someone who has sat through many, many presentations, I assure you that audiences will never complain if the presentation takes less time than scheduled; they will complain—and should—if it takes longer. For the presentations I'm invited to give, I usually request more time than I need and I make it a point to finish early. In this way, audiences feel they're getting away with something. They like that. No matter how much time I'm given, no matter how many questions I receive, I assume total responsibility for *ending the presentation when I said I would,* even if it means cutting material from my presentation.

Yes, but what if the time set aside for the presentation does not allow you to meet your objective? Here are a few options:

◆ Settle for a less ambitious, but more realistic, objective. Schedule a second presentation or arrange for a follow-up meeting.

◆ Provide an introductory handout a couple of days before the presentation that gives the audience preliminary information. Refer to it and *summarize* its highlights during the presentation for those who may not have read it. I emphasize the word *summarize.* Don't repeat the content of the handout page-by-page lest you be embarrassed the way one speaker was. When it became apparent that he was simply going to replay the advance handout, the decision maker in the audience said, "You can assume we read the handout. What we'd like to do today is decide what we're going to do about it." Ouch!

◆ As an alternative, let the audience know that additional information is in a handout they'll receive at the end of the presentation. (If at all possible, avoid distributing handouts at the beginning of the presentation; you run the risk of diverting the audience's attention from you and what you're presenting.)

◆ Prepare *backup* visuals for details or background information, and hold them in reserve in case the audience wants to know more—for example, the assumptions behind forecast data.

◆ Set priorities for segments of your presentation and for the visuals you plan to show: No. 1 for those that must be presented, No. 2 for those that can be omitted.

◆ Make a new agreement with the audience. I can think of one occasion when the audience was so full of questions that it became clear I could not finish on time without leaving many of the individuals in the room feeling incomplete. I paused, and I offered a new agreement: "Let's take a few moments to allow those who have other commitments to leave. For those who choose to remain, I'll stay as long as you have questions." One-third of the audience left. I spent another half hour with those who stayed.

Even when time is not an issue, it's a good idea to limit the amount of detail included. One of my friends calls our tendency to show everything we produced the "APK" syndrome, the *anxious parade of knowledge*. After about 40 minutes, the line charts all begin to look like bowls of spaghetti, and the pie charts conjure visions of dessert.

We can be reasonably sure that you'll be on time to begin the presentation. What if the audience isn't? What then?

Start the presentation on time. Maybe, just maybe, you can wait 3 to 5 minutes if the audience is settling down, but not much more; you owe it to those who are on time to *begin as scheduled.* After all, let's not punish those who are considerate enough to be on time for the sake of those who aren't, regardless of their status or their reason for being late.

Yes, but what if it's the decision maker who's late? *Start on time* and summarize what you've covered and where you are in the presentation once the latecomer(s) show up. I've come to realize that the audience members who are on time don't mind the interruption as much as they mind starting late.

I recall starting a presentation without one of the decision makers in the audience. She arrived 20 minutes late. I was proceeding as if nothing had happened when a member of the audience interrupted me to let me know that the rest of the audience could not reach consensus without the benefit of the latecomer's perspective. He asked me to take the time necessary to summarize the points I had made so far. As it turned out, with everyone on the same page, it was easier for me to gain the agreement I was asking for.

For me, starting on time and ending on time are more than matters of organization; they're matters of integrity. When we stay on schedule, we demonstrate our willingness and ability to keep our agreements and to meet our commitments.

WHAT MEDIUM SHOULD YOU USE?

If I had my way, the ideal medium would be universally available at any presentation site and simple to set up. It would be usable in a room of any size with room lights on. Its source of light would never burn out. It would use visual aids prepared from originals of any size that are inexpensive to produce, easy to revise, and produced with any available copying equipment. The visuals would be sharp and clear in color or black and white, and would be legible to an audience of any size from 1 to 1000. Dream on, Zelazny.

Because no medium with all those qualities exists, here's what's available for different situations, along with their pros and cons.

LAP VISUALS, so called because each member of the audience receives his or her own copy of the materials at the start of the meeting, if not earlier. Lap visuals are best used to generate interaction with not more than four people. Typically, the purpose is to discuss work to date, to check on the accuracy of facts, to surface issues, to test conclusions, to build consensus for recommendations, and to gain commitment for action programs.

The advantage of using lap visuals is that everyone feels like an equal partner in the discussion. Also, the audience members can write notes directly on the visuals, and they can flip the pages back and forth as they choose.

The disadvantage is that the audience may read ahead to pages you're not yet ready to discuss, which may lead to questions you would prefer to deal with later in the discussion. Also, with everyone looking down at his or her copy, you may miss the eye contact you need to make sure the audience members understand the points you're making.

Refer to the appendix, "Say It with Lap Visuals," for a more detailed description of this form of presentation.

EASELS OR ELECTRONIC WHITE BOARDS come in handy for discussions. In interactive meetings, recording the ideas as they come up gives the audience a feeling of participation. It lends a spontaneity to the discussion that can be highly energizing.

On the other hand, you'd better have a neat, legible handwriting; be able to write quickly; and keep the visuals simple, lest you spend more time with your back to the audience writing on the easel than discussing the thoughts with the audience. If only for reasons of legibility, I would limit the use of this medium to groups of not more than 15 people. Beyond that size, I recommend the use of projectors.

OVERHEAD TRANSPARENCIES are best for audiences of four to I'm not sure where to set the upper limit. I've used them successfully for audiences as large as 700. If you insist on an upper limit, I'd say about 40.

What I particularly like about this medium is that I can change the sequence of the visuals, I can omit transparencies, I can add backup visuals more easily than with any other medium, and I can write on blank transparencies to capture a spontaneous thought. Also, I really appreciate the ability to keep the room lights on. Together, these advantages give me the flexibility I feel I need for the interaction most business situations call for.

I can't think of much that's negative about overhead projectors. Because conference centers and corporations now stock these routinely, the fact that they aren't as portable as manufacturers would have you believe is not a problem. Also, office copiers make it easy to produce inexpensive transparencies in black and white, and the cost of color is coming down as well.

35-MM SLIDES are best used with audiences of more than, say, 40 people. In this situation, you usually stand at a lectern equipped with a microphone. With audiences of 20 to 50 people, you can use either 35-mm slides or transparencies, depending on the amount of interaction you want.

Unlike overhead projectors, 35-mm equipment allows you to change from one visual to the next with the use of a remote control. However, you're confined to the sequence of slides in the carousel tray. Also, the room must be somewhat darkened unless the screen is set up in a rear-projection arrangement (that's where the projector is behind a translucent screen). As a result, 35-mm presentations are best reserved for more formal presentations or speeches where you might expect little interaction with the audience.

Since I began to put these thoughts together, **COMPUTER TECHNOLOGY, LCD PROJECTORS, MULTIMEDIA,** *and all that jazz* have largely replaced the modes of presentation that I just discussed. They have certainly replaced 35-mm slides, and in no time at all, as the projection technology improves, they'll replace overhead transparencies as well.

Interestingly enough, I can't find agreement for what to call this presentation medium. Some call it *online*, some call it *new media,* others refer to it as *computer-based.* I'm calling it *onscreen.* When it incorporates animation, sound, and video, the consensus is to call it *multimedia.*

Here's the range of possibilities that can be created with this technology. These printed pages limit what I can demonstrate, but you'll get an idea of what can be done by following this progression of applications, each of which adds a higher level of sophistication to your presentations.

WE START WITH BASIC ONSCREEN PRESENTATION

Add animation. You can add motion and direction to your visuals by "zooming in or out," "wiping up or down," "dissolving" shapes or objects. For example, you can show the movement of goods in a process or the flow of responsibility in an organization chart.

Add scanned images. It's easy to scan commercially available colored pictures of products or of people into the visuals. Also, with the use of digital cameras, you can take the picture you want, import it into the computer, and modify it as you need to.

Add sound. How about the ring of a telephone or the honk of a car horn to add reality to the pictures you're showing? How about hearing a series of quotes endorsing a new idea, or listening to music to create a mood?

Add video. How about inserting a video clip of the scene you're describing: the bottleneck in the production line, the salesperson making a sale?

Add links. Link the product to its manufacturing source by making it possible to click on its URL to learn the details as published on the manufacturer's Web site. Link to a software program that lets you create on-the-spot calculations for alternative scenarios.

All in all, an impressive series of techniques that can contribute significantly to the success of your presentations. As you'd expect, there are pros and cons to be aware of.

The single most important benefit of onscreen presentation techniques is that they let you make changes to the visuals *during* the presentation, or between meetings while you're traveling from one presentation site to another, which allows you to add timely content and create what-if scenarios.

Because these presentations enable nonlinear branching into content, one presentation can serve multiple audiences in multiple ways. With little effort, you can start with the recommendations with an audience who will be receptive, or leave the recommendations to the end of the presentation for an audience who may be resistant.

For certain, the mix of video, sound, animation, and special effects makes for more engaging communication that can improve retention.

On the debit side, the equipment is not nearly as simple to set up as, for instance, overhead projectors, which require only a single wire plugged into the wall outlet. Trying to wire the laptop to the LCD projector and both to power sources, turning the equipment on in the right sequence, replicating the image from the laptop to the projector, . . . and so on, is the greatest test of patience, and currently one of the major reasons some presenters are reluctant to adopt the new technology.

Unless expertly handled, the constant parade of visuals can limit the interaction so important to business presentations. This happens because the focus is more on the *visuals* on the screen than it is on *you* the speaker.

Depending on the audience, the use of animations, dissolves, wipes, flying arrows, and so on, might appear to be gimmicky, giving the impression that you're spending time and money just to make your visuals flashier than they need to be to get your messages across—that you value form over content.

Given the pros and cons of these media options, here are the commandments I recommend to make the most of *all* media.

THE 10 COMMANDMENTS OF MEDIA

CREATING VISUALS

I Thou shalt keep the design of visuals simple. Omit footnotes and sources for charts; limit the number of words on text visuals to 30.

II Thou shalt ensure legibility to the person sitting the farthest from the screen. Take a look at the detailed table included in the section on legibility.

III Thou shalt use color with purpose, not for decoration. Use color to emphasize, to identify a recurring theme, to distinguish, or to symbolize.

IV Thou shalt keep special effects (*e.g., animations*) to a minimum and let content drive their use.

V Thou shalt provide reasonable production deadlines. As more elements, such as video and sound, are added, presentations are more time-consuming, and more expensive to produce.

PRESENTING

VI Thou shalt rehearse, rehearse, rehearse before the presentation; during is too late. You'll be more relaxed during the presentation if you're thoroughly familiar with it and if you've anticipated questions before the presentation.

VII Thou shalt arrive extra early at the presentation site and work closely with the technical professional. Make sure audio and video playback and software are compatible; room lights are properly adjusted to make it dark around the screen and as light as possible in the rest of the room; you know whom to call in case anything goes wrong during the presentation. Better yet, ask the specialist to be in the room.

VIII Thou shalt bring backup visuals. You can seldom go far enough to protect against the unexpected.

IX Thou shalt project a blank screen during lengthy transitions, while answering audience's questions, or entering into a discussion. A blank screen ensures that the audience members focus on you without the distraction of the visual.

X Thou shalt try to follow 7 of the 10 Commandments most of the time.

DESIGN
THE PRESENTATION

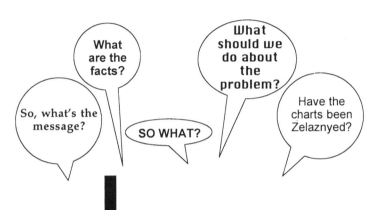

If you're like me, you can no longer count how many times you've wished for a magic formula that would make presentations simpler to prepare. Unfortunately, we've all seen too many that follow what's become the fallback formula, the kind of presentation that I hope to erase from the conference rooms of the universe. It goes like this:

| TITLE PHRASE FINDER | Step 1: Select at random a 3-digit number |
| | Step 2: Match the digits to the columns |

COLUMN A		COLUMN B		COLUMN C	
0	ASSESSING	0	STRATEGIC	0	EFFECTIVENESS
1	DEVELOPING	1	ORGANIZATIONAL	1	OPPORTUNITIES
2	STRENGTHENING	2	OPERATIONAL	2	CAPABILITIES
3	IMPROVING	3	STRATEGIC	3	PRIORITIES
4	MANIPULATING	4	ORGANIZATIONAL	4	RESOURCES
5	IN SEARCH OF	5	OPERATIONAL	5	MANAGEMENT
6	IMPLEMENTING	6	STRATEGIC	6	EXCELLENCE
7	NURTURING	7	ORGANIZATIONAL	7	ALTERNATIVES
8	INSTITUTIONALIZING	8	OPERATIONAL	8	CHALLENGES
9	REVITALIZING	9	EVERYTHING ELSE	9	COMPETITIVENESS

THE ALL-PURPOSE PRESENTATION

Visual number one: the title. It occurs to me that most presenters have run out of original titles. Their titles all seem to come from this handy *Title Phrase Finder.*

33

BACKGROUND

About _____ ☐ days, ☐ weeks, ☐ months, ☐ years ago,

you asked us to _____

Fill in title of presentation

_____ of your company

Next, of course, these presenters feel the need to let the audience know how long they've been working on the project, whether it's relevant or irrelevant. This visual is designed to do that.

WHAT WE DID

To familiarize ourselves with your operations we interviewed

☐ Members of Board of Directors   ☐ Division managers

☐ Presidents   ☐ Regional managers

☐ Executive vice presidents   ☐ Area managers

☐ Plain vice presidents   ☐ Salesman or agents

☐ Junior vice presidents   ☐ Others

To impress the audience, the same presenters often describe the pain they went through to prepare for today's presentation. They elaborate on the number of interviews they conducted . . .

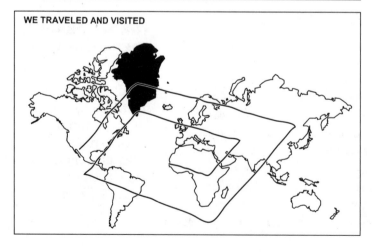

WE TRAVELED AND VISITED

. . . the places they visited to uncover what's happening.

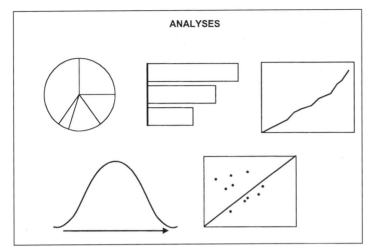

ANALYSES

Then they start sharing the many sophisticated analyses they performed—visuals numbers 7–144.

Finally, 1 hour and 45 minutes later, they reveal their conclusions and recommendations to an audience that's either dozing, fidgeting, or gone.

There's a better way, however. A presentation should answer a question for the audience—the question your project was designed to resolve. It should answer that question in a way that helps the audience see the reasons for the answer. In this chapter, I talk about how to do that. First, I explain why and how to *define your message*. Then I discuss how to *craft the story line, introduction, and ending* so they support the message and hold the audience's attention. I follow up with how to *design visuals* that bring the story line to life.

DETERMINE YOUR MESSAGE

Let's say for the moment that your client invites you to give a presentation to the executive committee on the project you've been working on for the past 6 months. In the process of discussing the details, the client realizes that this is an important meeting and allots 4 hours for your presentation.

You proceed to put together 4 hours' worth of presentation. Four hours' worth of cardboard-framed overhead transparencies is about 2 feet high. You walk into the conference room balancing the 2-foot pile of transparencies, drop them on the conference room table, and your client says, "Oops, sorry, I know I said you'd have 4 hours, but we have a crisis and we can give you only 1 minute."

"One minute!" the voice in your head screeeeeeeeeeaaaaams. Now, after that little silent voice goes through every dirty word in its vocabulary for 30 seconds, what would you say, in the remaining 30 seconds that would summarize the 4-hour presentation? **THAT'S YOUR MESSAGE.**

It doesn't matter how complex your presentation is; there's nothing that can't be summarized in 30 seconds to a minute when you have to. Think about television commercials, one of the most powerful forms of communication we're exposed to every day, and you realize that most of them last 30 seconds. *(I know you'll appreciate, as I do, the talent, creativity—yes, and money—that goes into producing them. All for a 30-second message. Brilliant forms of presentation. Study them.)*

Determining your message calls for a bumper sticker mentality:

Honk if you're from Da Bronx.

You want a message that's like a newspaper headline—a statement that captures your interest and makes you want to read more:

European air fares start falling out of the sky.

Although these examples are good starting points, in a business presentation, the message must be broadened sufficiently to lead the listener toward the details of the solution. Here, it's the answer to the question you were asked to probe. It's the unifying element of your presentation, the *what's so* and the *so what* in one minute:

To counter the limited potential for growth at home, J.J. Ltd. should proceed with its efforts to tap the significant growth opportunities in the United States.

Write your message down and keep it in a prominent place as you move to develop the story line of the presentation. That, combined with your objective—what you want your audience to do about the message—will keep your energy focused on making sure that the presentation is successful.

Applying what I preach. If I had only 1 minute of your time and I had to single out the one suggestion that would heighten the success of your presentations, it would be this: Start your presentation by saying, "If I had only 1 minute of your time today, this is what I'd like you to get from my presentation . . . ," and then tell them your message. End the thought with, "Fortunately, you've given me 4 hours, so for the next 3 hours and 59 minutes, I'll give you the full picture."

Use this approach and you may never have to give the 3-hour-and-59-minute version. I realize that you may not appreciate this result, considering all the work you put into getting ready for the presentation. On the other hand, think how grateful your audience will be. I believe if we used this approach more often, and spent the rest of the time answering questions, we would finish sooner, and no member of the audience would complain.

CRAFT THE STORY LINE

When it comes to discussing the story line of your presentation, I feel like the Antonio Salieri to the Amadeus Mozart of the field. In this case, Amadeus is Barbara Minto, founder and author of *The Pyramid Principle*.[2] Do yourself a favor and order a copy of her book, in which she presents the process for synthesizing facts and ideas so they lead to logical conclusions. My goal here is not to repeat her tested and vibrant ideas on structure, but to share my observations and experience on how to position your conclusions once you've surfaced them.

When the time comes to report on our projects, we have a tendency to re-create the problem-solving approach we used—be it the chronology of events we followed, or the sequence of analyses we used—to come up with the conclusions, and subsequently, with the recommendations. My experience has been that it's best to begin the presentation with your recommendation—the message you just wrote down—and use the time you have left telling the

---

[2]Barbara Minto, *The Pyramid Principle,* Copyright 1998, Barbara Minto International, 19 Cadogan Place, Bell 3, London SWIX 9 SA, England.

audience why you think that's the best answer to the issue you were asked to resolve.

Take a look at this simple example that shows the difference. Here is a letter from Shirley's dearest friend. For a few seconds I'd like you to become Shirley and get in touch with your thoughts as you figure out what Lucy is trying to tell you.

Dear Shirley,

Remember last Saturday afternoon when I was playing in the park with my boyfriend and you came over, and he told me that when my back was turned, you kissed him?

And also, on Sunday when you came to my house and my Mom made you a tuna fish salad for lunch and you said: "Yech! That's the worst salad I ever ate!"?

And yesterday, when my cat brushed against your leg, you kicked her and threatened to sic your dog "Monster" on her?

Well, for all of these reasons, I hate you, and I no longer want to be your friend.

Lucy

Notice that when you read the first paragraph, about something that happened last Saturday, you weren't clear where the letter was leading. So you read the second paragraph, about something that happened Sunday, and then on to what happened yesterday. And, if you add the first paragraph to the second, and to the third, you can see how it leads to the eventual punch line.

Granted, that's the chronology in which the events took place. Notice how much more clearly the point of the letter comes across, how much more forceful the letter is, how much simpler it is, and how much more impact it has if you rewrite it from the bottom up, putting your conclusions first.

Dear Shirley,

I HATE you. Here are my reasons:

1. You stole my boyfriend.

2. You insulted my mother.

3. You scared my cat.

Now, I wouldn't recommend such a blunt approach for a social relationship, but let's apply the principle to a business example. Here we're making a presentation to the board of an English bank that needs to decide whether to enter the U.S. market.

Play the following game with me for a few minutes. I'm appointing you to be a member of this board. The price you have to pay is to sit through the presentation—or at least, its outline—and to decide, not so much whether it's a good idea, but, for the sake of the exercise, which story line gets its message across to you with the least mental gymnastics. (*Bear in mind that the outline is much more concise than the full presentation, which would contain the facts supporting each statement in the outline.*)

Let's start with a story line that reflects the problem-solving approach to deciding whether entering the United States is wise. Based on the positioning of the conclusions, nod at the point you think you know for certain whether the recommendation is "Go/No Go."

OBJECTIVE	To determine whether J.J. Ltd. should proceed with efforts to capitalize on U.S. opportunities
TOPIC **A**	**U.S. role in world's economy**
Evidence	1. Largest share of world's GNP 2. Most foreign trade 3. Expected increase in foreign investment
TOPIC **B**	**Attractiveness of U.S. industry returns**
Evidence	4. Rigorous cost control 5. Solid competitive position 6. Etc.
TOPIC **C**	**Barriers to entry**
Evidence	7. Markets fragmented 8. Customers receptive
Summary of CONCLUSIONS	**A. United States is the world's leading economy.** **B. U.S. industry returns are attractive.** **C. Barriers to entry can be overcome.**
RECOMMENDATION	**PROCEED!**

Chances are that it took you at least to the summary of conclusions before you knew for certain the action called for. In the full presentation, that would be at least 45 minutes, and maybe a lot longer.

Let's continue the game. This time, I thought about the second letter to Shirley as I prepared for the presentation. Once more, read through and nod when you know the recommendation.

RECOMMENDATION	**J.J. Ltd. should proceed with efforts to capitalize on U.S. opportunities**
Preview of CONCLUSIONS	**A. The United States is the world's leading economy.**
	B. U.S. industry returns are attractive.
	C. Barriers to entry can be overcome.
CONCLUSION **A**	**The United States is the world's leading economy.**
Evidence	1. Largest share of world's GNP 2. Most foreign trade 3. Expected increase in foreign investment
CONCLUSION **B**	**U.S. industry returns are attractive.**
Evidence	4. Rigorous cost control 5. Solid competitive position 6. Etc.
CONCLUSION **C**	**Barriers to entry can be overcome.**
Evidence	7. Markets fragmented 8. Customers receptive
RECOMMENDATION	**PROCEED!**

Didn't take very long, did it? You knew the recommendation right away.

Now you're certainly not convinced just because you know the recommendation in the first few moments. That's what the rest of the presentation is designed for: to give you the conclusions that led to the recommendation and the evidence that supports those conclusions. However, because you know what the conclusions are, you can evaluate the strength of the evidence as you learn it. You, the audience, are not simply passive recipients of facts, but an active participant in a process of reasoning.

Okay, I hear you. What if the audience is not in an agreeing mood? What if the recommendation isn't what they want to hear? What if they're hostile? What if you're working with individuals whose life's work is based on building the arguments, from facts to conclusions to recommendations? Well, one thing you can do is be just a little less forthcoming with the conclusions. Don't save them for the very end, but reserve them for the end of each section. Like this:

OBJECTIVE	**To determine whether J.J. Ltd. should proceed with efforts to capitalize on U.S. opportunities**
Preview of ISSUES	**A. Strength of the economy**
	B. Profit potential
	C. Feasibility
ISSUE **A**:	**Strength of economy**
Evidence	1. Largest share of world's GNP
	2. Most foreign trade
	3. Expected increase in foreign investment
CONCLUSION **A**	**The United States is the world's leading economy.**
ISSUE **B**:	**Profit potential**
Evidence	4. Rigorous cost control
	5. Solid competitive position
	6. Etc.

CONCLUSION **B**	**U.S. industry returns are attractive.**
ISSUE **C**:	**Feasibility**
Evidence	7. Markets fragmented
	8. Customers receptive
CONCLUSION **C**	**Barriers to entry can be overcome.**
Summary of CONCLUSIONS	**A. The United States is the world's leading economy.**
	B. U.S. industry returns are attractive.
	C. Barriers to entry can be overcome.
RECOMMENDATION	**PROCEED!**

While delaying the conclusion until the end of each section serves its purpose well in the situations that call for it, I would nonetheless argue that for 90 percent of the presentations you give, you're better off leading with the recommendation or, at the very least, with the conclusions. If you remain uncomfortable given your understanding of the audience's possible reaction, then you may have to hold your conclusions and recommendation for the end of the presentation, but that's rarely the best way to go. Even when you know the audience is going to be resistant, I would rather hear you say something like this in the introduction:

"Good morning . . . We're about to present a recommendation we know you're *not* going to like. We want you to know that the team spent a lot of time thinking about the problem. We studied all the possible options and spent many hours discussing the pros and cons. We would not be presenting this answer if we felt there was another recourse. We recommend that you proceed with efforts to tap the growth opportunities in the United States. In the rest of the presentation, we'll explain why."

In other words, make the members of the audience feel that you have anticipated their reaction and are sensitive to their feelings. Put yourself in the audience's seat as you listen to that introduction and decide how you would feel.

Conclusions/recommendation up front? In the middle? At the end? The answer depends on how you defined the situation and especially on how receptive you think the audience members will be. Once you've made this choice, you're ready to develop the introduction and ending that will bracket the presentation.

WRITE THE INTRODUCTION

Think back to the plane flights you've taken. What do you do in the first minutes of the flight when the airline attendant introduces you to the safety features of the plane? If you're like me, you go unconscious: You close your ears, you turn off your mind, you doze off.

So it is with many presentations; the introduction lulls me to sleep.

Now, what would happen if the ship's officer were to announce:

Ladies and gentlemen, if you look through the windows on the right of the plane, you'll notice a fire has developed in engine number four!

You'd be quick to pay full attention. Chances are you would silence any other passenger who tried to get in the way of the questions you want answered.

That's what introductions need to do: They need to light a fire under the audience, to arouse enthusiasm for being there, to build anticipation for what's going to follow.

I leave it to your imagination to find a way to light the fire. As for introducing the content, the formula I use is **PIP:**

♦ **P for purpose.** Why are you giving this presentation? Why are we here? What will success look like at the end of the presentation?

♦ **I for importance.** What makes it so important that we accomplish *that* purpose today? What's the relevance of this presentation to the problems we face? What's the urgency?

♦ **P for preview.** Give us a bird's-eye view of the way the presentation is structured, of what to anticipate during the time we're going to spend together, so that we can concentrate on content and not on questioning where we are in the presentation.

You can present the elements of the **PIP** formula in any sequence, depending on the tone you feel you need to establish. You can tell me, for example:

> **Purpose:** "My purpose today is to present a portfolio of practical suggestions to help you overcome the nervousness that comes with delivering presentations." **Importance:** "This is most timely, because you'll be presenting your recommendations to the Community Board next week." **Preview:** "In the hour we have together, we'll discuss the steps required to plan, design, and deliver successful presentations."

Or

> **Importance:** "You've been invited to present your recommendations to the Community Board next week." **Purpose:** "Therefore, I want to spend the next hour giving you a portfolio of practical suggestions to overcome the nervousness that comes with delivering presentations." **Preview:** "Let me begin by discussing how to plan for the presentation, and follow it up with the steps involved in

designing it, and close with ideas for how to deliver it successfully."

Or

Preview: "In this presentation, I'll discuss the steps required to plan, design, and deliver any presentation." **Purpose:** "As you know, delivering presentations can generate a lot of nervous tension. Therefore, my purpose is to show you how the steps we'll be discussing can help you cope with the nervous energy." **Importance:** "This discussion is most timely, because you've been asked to present your recommendations to the Community Board next week."

As you think about how to construct your **PIP** introduction, remember that audience members have a lot on their minds as they sit to listen to your presentation. Make sure the introduction is structured in a way that will shift their attention to what you're about to present. Make them feel that what you have to say is well worth their time and attention.

It's a good idea to write the introduction in advance, to be sure that you think through the flow and tone.

PLAN THE ENDING

Few things bring a smile to your audience's face more quickly than the words ". . . and to summarize." Even if your presentation is clear, interesting, and well structured, your audience will appreciate being freed to return to their other responsibilities. The ending, like the introduction, is where the audience's attention is at its highest. Here's what I recommend for an effective ending:

1. **Summarize the major points** you made in the presentation, be they conclusions, trends, arguments, whatever.

2. **Spell out the recommendation** one more time. (*Remember, you introduced it as* the main message *of the presentation.*)

3. **Present your action program.** The audience is more likely to agree with your recommendation once they see that you have anticipated what it will take to implement it. Include a chart that shows the specific steps or actions required to make the recommendation happen. Identify who will be respon-

sible for each step. Show how much time each step will take, and, as a result, when to expect final implementation. Indicate how much each step will cost, and what the total budget will look like.

4. **Ask for agreement and for commitment** to make the recommendations happen. Don't mistake nods of the head or statements such as "I understand" throughout the presentation to mean, "We agree." Be bold, be direct, be specific. Ask: "Our objective today was to get your agreement to cutting cost in your department by 30 percent. Have we done so, and can we expect to see results at the end of the fiscal quarter?" If the audience doesn't agree, enter into a discussion of what needs to be done to gain their approval.

5. **Close off with "next steps."** Summarize all the agreements that were made during the presentation. For instance, someone from the audience asked for a special analysis; you asked for additional information. Repeat those at the end to assure the involved individuals that you heard them. Also, gain agreement for subsequent meetings or presentations.

A presentation doesn't necessarily end with the last words spoken. A presentation is often only one event in a series of events that establishes a relationship between you and the members of the audience. The ending should signal that everyone is looking forward to working together in the future.

MAKE THE MOST OF VISUALS

I'm going to skip the lengthy commercial that convinces you that visuals are important. Suffice it to say that they have the ability to demonstrate relationships more clearly and more quickly than information in words or tables.

This chart identifies the range of visuals that are available. At the top are text visuals, which are used to explain what and why. To the left are the quantitative charts, and to the right, conceptual charts. Along with these are the pictures, photographs, images, models, and videos that should be considered part of today's visual vocabulary.

The question I want to address here is not why visuals are important, but how to design them. First we'll discuss charts, both quantitative and conceptual, then we'll look at text visuals. I'll finish with a sermon about legibility.

Narrative

What? Why?

Words words words
Words words words
Words words words
Words words words

Quantitative

— **How much?** —

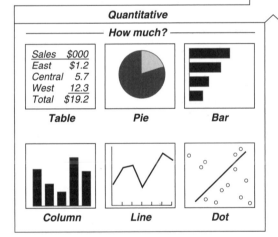

Table	Pie	Bar
Column	Line	Dot

Non-quantitative

Who?	Where?	When?

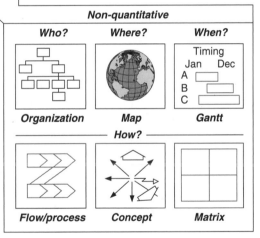

Organization	Map	Gantt

— **How?** —

Flow/process	Concept	Matrix

DESIGNING CHARTS FOR THE ZEN OF IT

For the step-by-step process of translating data into charts, I refer you to my book, *Say It with Charts*. For now, I'd like to try a different approach with you. The approach is triggered by the answer that only a Zen master could have come up with when asked, "Do you know how to play the violin?" Answer, "I don't know, I never tried."

And so, let me ask you, "Do you know how to design charts?"

Whether you've tried or not, I believe you do know, and if you've tried and think you can't, it doesn't mean you can't; it means you *think* you can't. I believe it's probably more a matter of confidence than skill. Here, in the privacy of this book, you can discover that you do know how to draw charts without the fear of getting it wrong.

Now the truth is that I don't know any Zen masters on whom to test my premise. The closest test case I can think of is a 6-year-old child. So let me call on that little 6-year-old inside you, the one who learned to ride a bike before you knew there were instruction manuals; the one who knew how to hit a tennis ball before you were told that you didn't know how to hold the racquet; the one who did things because you wanted to and not because there were reasons, logic, processes, rules, steps, procedures, and right and wrong that you had to think about to do them correctly.

Here goes: Take a colored crayon in hand and sketch the *very, very, very first* image that comes to you for each of the eight messages on the following pages. Remember that crayons don't have erasers, so only your first idea counts— you can't change your mind. Furthermore, if you're 6 years old, you've very impatient, so don't spend much time with each—if the answer doesn't come up for you quickly, move on to the next message. Most important, of course, is that at 6, you don't know you have a mind, so you don't think—you just do. So *do it!*

Afterward, compare what you've done with what other children like you have drawn and discover that you've designed charts that are every bit as good as anybody else's. It's a matter of trusting yourself.

1 Company sales have increased four times since 1990.

2 Company A has the smallest share of the industry.

3 The project will advance in five phases.

4 Client's ROS ranks fourth.

❶ Company sales have increased four times since 1990.

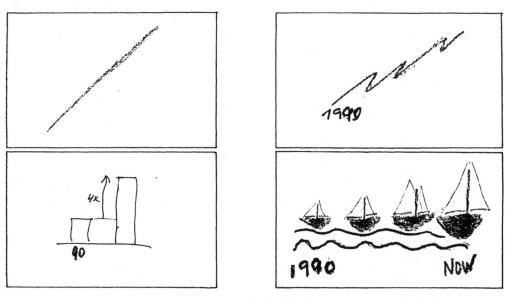

1. It doesn't matter whether you use a line chart or a bar chart. In each case the audience sees that something is moving up, and that's the message. (I'd guess that the last visual was drawn by the son of a rich executive.)

2 Company A has the smallest share of the industry.

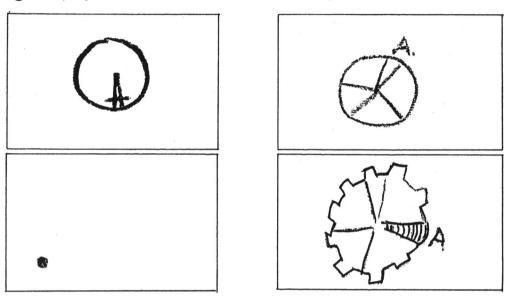

2. "Company A has the smallest *share of* . . ." I'll bet you drew some form of a pie chart. Most people do when they see the words *share of* anything.

❸ The project will advance in five phases.

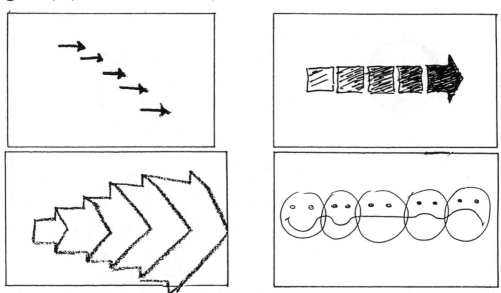

3. Because arrows show movement and direction, they are ideal for visualizing successive phases over time. I'm showing off with the last representation—the one showing the five faces. It's my all-time favorite. I drew it for Nancy when she came into my office needing to present the results of a study she had been leading for the past few months. She wanted to describe what happened to the morale of employees as they joined a particular company—two months before joining, two weeks before, the day they joined, two weeks after, and two months later.

4 Client's ROS ranks fourth.

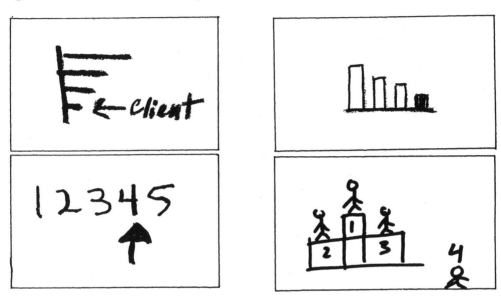

4. It doesn't matter whether we know what ROS means; that's not what we're visualizing. What we're visualizing is something *ranking fourth.* Whether we draw a bar chart, or a column chart, or leave the data in tabular form is immaterial; in all these sketches, we clearly see the message being supported by the visuals.

5 The age distribution of company employees differs sharply from that of its competitors.

6 House buyers are caught in the crisscross of decreased construction and increased building costs.

7 The five programs are interrelated.

8 The two project teams must interact for better results.

5 The age distribution of company employees differs sharply from that of its competitors.

5. Whether you show a line chart or a column chart or a pie chart doesn't matter in this case; they all work equally well to show the age comparisons. On the other hand, don't lose sight of the audience you're addressing. Where the conventional charts would work well in a presentation to management, the birthday cakes would work better if you were presenting to a class of elementary school children.

6 House buyers are caught in the crisscross of decreased construction and increased building costs.

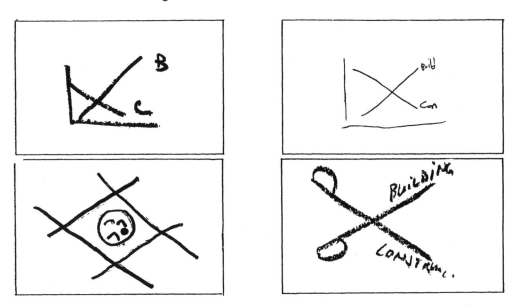

6. The magic word in the title is *crisscross;* that's what needs to be visualized. By the way, the images need not be limited to abstract shapes. In this case, the image of the scissors does a good job of reinforcing the effect of being caught in a crisscross.

7 The five programs are interrelated.

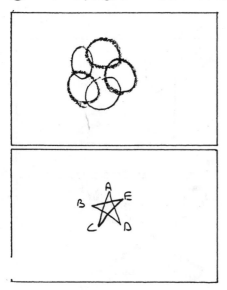

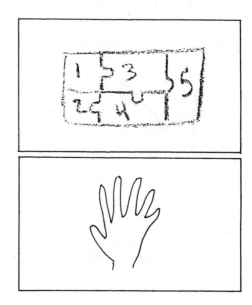

7. I've used the image of a puzzle many times to show interrelationships. Each piece can be discussed independently, and showing the pieces together depicts how they must fit to work together successfully. (I found the last one most interesting; this six-year-old child has six fingers.)

8 The two project teams must interact for better results.

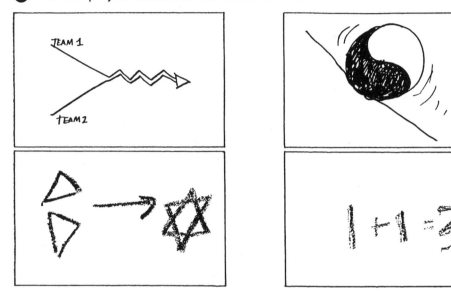

8. The idea of interacting, of working together, is clearly demonstrated by any of these, be it the Yin Yang symbol, or the two independent triangles working together to become the Star of David, or the synergy created by 1 plus 1 equaling more than the sum of its parts.

9 The task forces are moving in opposite directions.

10 Range of discounts offered for the new model varies widely by geographic area.

11 Forces at work on the company will result in restructuring.

12 The trend follows a vicious circle.

9 The task forces are moving in opposite directions.

9. These pictures speak louder than any words I could say.

10 Range of discounts offered for the new model varies widely by geographic area

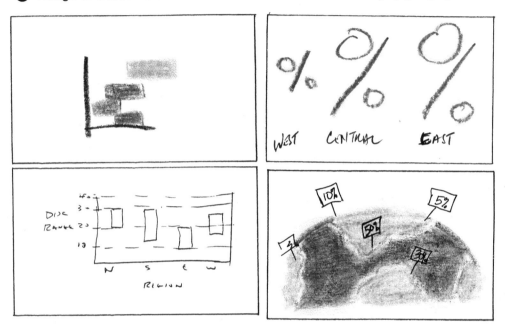

10. Here, you probably focused either on the range of discounts with bars or columns, or on the geographic areas, or a combination. I found the % signs of different sizes original.

11 Forces at work on the company will result in restructuring.

11. Notice in the upper right illustration how the three arrows suggest the forces at work on the circle (i.e., the company), and how, then, the arrow pointing to the right leads to the idea of taking action as a result of the pressures. On the other hand, the battle between Luke Skywalker and Darth Vader says it more imaginatively.

⓬ The trend follows a vicious circle.

12. I doubt that your vicious circle is anywhere near as vicious as these.

*　　*　　*

Next time you're designing charts, trust your intuition. Call on the six-year-old you were, and if you *visualize the message, not the mess,* your charts will improve. Who knows, you might even discover that you know how to play the violin. For now, I owe you a lollipop.

DESIGNING TEXT VISUALS

Let's go back in history for a while, for instance, back to the Roman era where we wait for Marc Antony to deliver his eulogy to Julius Caesar. There he is, in his best Sunday toga, walking up the steps of the Forum to make his presentation to the crowd. "We're all ears, Marc."

Marc begins, "Friends, Romans, Countrymen, lend me your ears . . ." However, this isn't Marc's usual fiery oration. Instead, Marc has had the script of his speech projected onto a bed sheet draped between two Corinthian columns. He has turned his back to the audience. He's reading his script—word for word.

As you'd expect, the Romans in the audience turned *their* backs on Marc and headed home after he started to read. Travel through time and you have a style of presentation that doesn't work for modern-day speakers either, but it persists. It's a style that relies on pages and pages of text written by presenters who don't trust themselves or who are more concerned about the handout than the presentation. It's a style that is more *recitation* than *presentation.*

Take a look at the following example. It's typical of the kind of text visuals we're all too often exposed to in the business world.

MAJOR WEAKNESSES IN THE ORGANIZATION

Stocks and Bonds' present management structure has several important deficiencies that should be corrected in any substantial realignment of responsibilities.

1. No single recognized head of the firm (i.e., Management Committee, CEO, CFO, COO).

2. No clearly defined lines of authority and responsibility for major activities or geographical locations.

3. A real conflict exists between the production department and the administration (e.g., who determines forecasts?).

4. Inadequate "thinking through" of how much autonomy should be granted to regions (or branches) in various phases of the firm's activities. What authority in each should be exercised by Corporate Headquarters?

What's wrong with using it as a presentation visual? The question is how to present it. If you read the words exactly as they appear on the visual, it doesn't take long before the members of the audience feel their intelligence is being insulted because you're reading to them what they can obviously read for themselves.

Another option is to paraphrase. The problem with paraphrasing is that few people can read one set of words while listening to another.

This leaves open the option of remaining quiet, giving the audience members a chance to read for themselves. Although that may work occasionally, after a while the silence in the room becomes awkward. Furthermore, it's hard to judge how long to be quiet to make sure that everyone, including us slow readers, has a chance to read all the points.

These problems don't mean that you should never use text visuals. Text visuals can be most effective when:

(a) They help the audience see the structure of a complex presentation, or of a chapter:

IMPROVING LIFECO'S PERFORMANCE

    1. Review industry trends.

    2. Assess Lifeco's performance.

    3. Present preliminary recommendations.

    4. Discuss next steps.

(b) They reinforce important sets of ideas such as three conclusions, four recommendations, five issues, six next steps:

RECOMMENDATIONS

    1. Establish relationship management system.

    2. Form dedicated service teams.

    3. Reconfigure sales office network.

    4. Organize around customer categories.

The long-form text I showed you earlier is a necessary first step to make sure that you know what you want to say, to provide you with reference notes during the presentation, and to create the version that you'll include in the handout to the audience. It's the *before*. The trick is to turn it into a brief presentation visual by:

Distinguishing what should be **said** from what should be **shown**

Eliminating parenthetical comments, such as *e.g.*s or *i.e.*s

Editing the sentences from eight words to five, five words to four, and so on

Here I show all that can be eliminated in the process of translating the long form into the short form that should be used for the presentation.

MAJOR WEAKNESSES IN THE ORGANIZATION

Stocks and Bonds' present management structure has several important deficiencies that should be corrected in any substantial realignment of responsibilities.

1. No single recognized head of the firm (that is, Management Committee, CEO, CFO, COO).

2. No clearly defined lines of authority and responsibility for major activities or geographical locations.

3. A real conflict exists between the production department and the administration (for example, who determines forecasts?).

4. Inadequate thinking through of how much autonomy should be granted to regions (or branches) in various phases of the firm's activities, and what authority in each should be exercised by Corporate Headquarters.

Here's the *after*.

ORGANIZATION WEAKNESSES

1. **No single recognized head of firm**

2. **No clear authority and responsibility**

3. **Conflict between production and administration**

4. **Tension between regional autonomy and corporate authority**

Now you are no longer a prisoner of the words on the screen; you can elaborate in as much—or as little—detail as you need to. As a result, you can spend time with your audience rather than looking at the screen for word cues, and you have created the space on the visual to make it legible.

Better yet, take the next step and translate the text visual into what I call a *structure visual*. As with charts, words merely imply the relationships among the ideas, whereas a visual demonstrates them.

For example, here's a text visual, which identifies the four steps to innovation to be discussed in a presentation.

THE INNOVATION PROCESS

1. **Create a vision**

2. **Generate insights**

3. **Establish priorities**

4. **Execute successfully**

The text visual works well enough, but notice how much more effective it becomes when shown as a structure visual that demonstrates the relationship among the steps. If nothing else, it creates a more memorable visual, which will stand out from the crowd of other text visuals in the presentation.

THE INNOVATION PROCESS

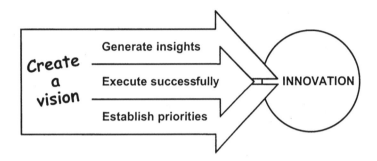

For a rich vocabulary of visual images you can use to translate text pages into structure visuals, refer to the last chapter of my other book, *Say It with Charts*, where I present "Solutions in Search of Problems."

ENSURING LEGIBILITY

Speaking of legibility, a few years ago, a friend of mine received this letter. (*As you'd expect, I changed the references.*) Under a magnifying glass here's what it said:

Dear name of company

Having trouble reading this, aren't you?

In the six months we have sat through your visual presentations, three members of our company have been fitted for bifocals, one has purchased a seeing-eye dog, and the chairman of our committee is now running a newsstand.

The letter goes on to beg for visuals that are legible. Although the letter is fun, the message is serious.

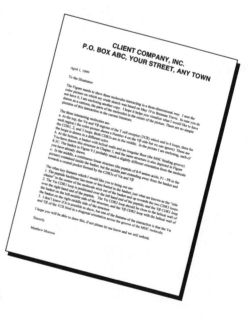

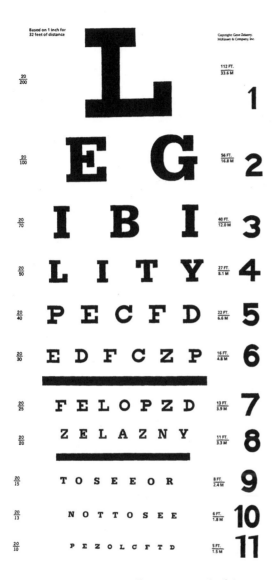

Based on 1 inch for
32 feet of distance

20/200	**L**	112 FT. / 33.6 M	**1**
20/100	**E G**	56 FT. / 16.8 M	**2**
20/70	**I B I**	40 FT. / 12.0 M	**3**
20/50	**L I T Y**	27 FT. / 8.1 M	**4**
20/40	**P E C F D**	22 FT. / 6.6 M	**5**
20/30	**E D F C Z P**	16 FT. / 4.8 M	**6**
20/25	**F E L O P Z D**	13 FT. / 3.9 M	**7**
20/20	**Z E L A Z N Y**	11 FT. / 3.3 M	**8**
20/15	T O S E E O R	8 FT. / 2.4 M	**9**
20/13	N O T T O S E E	6 FT. / 1.8 M	**10**
20/10	P E Z O L C F T D	5 FT. / 1.5 M	**11**

If it's important enough to be a visual, it's important enough to be legible. Do what my friend did: He charged the members of his staff $5 for every visual that was not legible. At the end of a month, he donated the proceeds to the Lighthouse, a not-for-profit agency that helps people who are blind or partially sighted.

Let me put it this way: No one will ever complain if the lettering is too big; all should if it's too small.

Sorry about the sermon.

81

Here's a table that shows how far from the screen a member of the audience can sit and find various type sizes comfortably legible on a 6-foot, 8-foot, or 12-foot screen. Allow for a 5 to 10 percent variance in legibility depending on the brightness of the projector, the contrast created by the darkness of the room, and the intensity of the image the closer the projector is to the screen.

MAXIMUM DISTANCE FROM SCREEN

Size of type	Width of screen		
	6 ft	8 ft	12 ft
16pt. lowercase	15 ft	18 ft	20 ft
18pt. lowercase	23	25	27
20pt. lowercase	30	35	45
22pt. lowercase	35	40	50
24pt. lowercase	45	50	60
30pt. lowercase	50	60	70
32pt. lowercase	62	70	80

BUILD A STORYBOARD

One of the finest tools for playing with the structure and design of the presentation is now available with the *storyboard* function of your graphics software package. The virtue of the tool is that it minimizes our tendency to get so wrapped up in the intricacies of a single chart that we fail to relate the visual to the total story. A storyboard lets us map out the flow of the presentation, relating each chart to the next until the sequence of ideas presented leads the audience to take the action we recommend. It lets us see where we have too many charts for a simple point and not enough for more complicated ones; it allows us to identify transition problems; and it helps us determine where we should summarize before introducing the next thought.

Here's how to do it:

1. **Draft the outline of your presentation,** following the story line you decided on, so that you know what you're going to present and in what order.

2. Following the outline, **decide where visuals are needed and what those visuals might look like.**

For example, you might want a text visual to introduce the structure of the presentation. Then, you might want a pie chart to illustrate the first finding that the "United States has the largest share of world's GDP," a bar chart to show that the "United States has more foreign trade than any other country," and a column chart to demonstrate the rise of foreign direct investment.

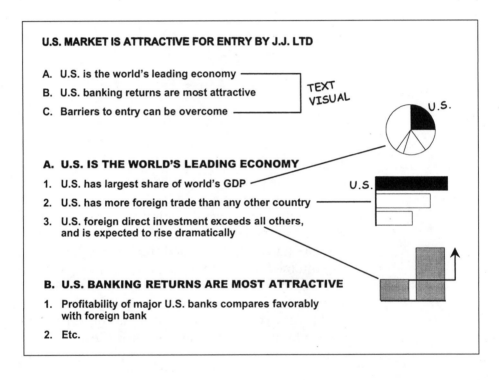

3. **Create the visuals.** To the right, or underneath the visual, write out what you're going to say when you present it, including how to read the visual and its "so what"—what makes it important to the story.

4. **Check the flow.** Test the logic of the sequence of the charts, decide where there are too many charts for a simple point and not enough for more compli-

cated ones, and determine where you need to summarize before moving on.

5. **Keep your medium in mind and note any animations** that will be included in the final production of your materials. *(I've created a shorthand visual language for indicating the most commonly used animations. You're welcome to use it—or create one of your own.)*

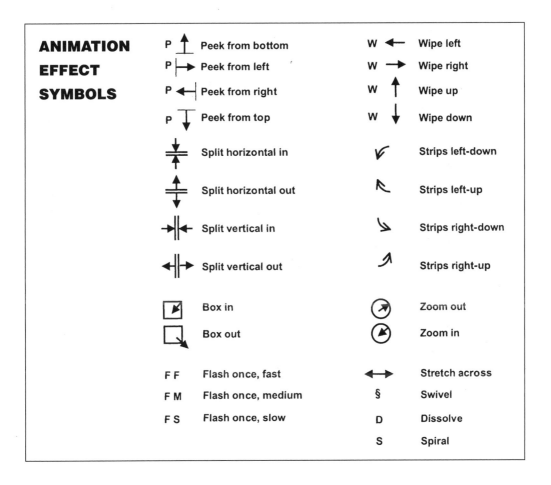

ANIMATION EFFECT SYMBOLS

Symbol	Description	Symbol	Description
P ↑	Peek from bottom	W ←	Wipe left
P ⊢→	Peek from left	W →	Wipe right
P ←⊣	Peek from right	W ↑	Wipe up
P ↓	Peek from top	W ↓	Wipe down
	Split horizontal in		Strips left-down
	Split horizontal out		Strips left-up
→‖←	Split vertical in		Strips right-down
←‖→	Split vertical out		Strips right-up
	Box in	⊙↗	Zoom out
	Box out	⊙↙	Zoom in
F F	Flash once, fast	↔	Stretch across
F M	Flash once, medium	§	Swivel
F S	Flash once, slow	D	Dissolve
		S	Spiral

By the way, don't worry about showing too many visuals. Some speakers equate the number of visuals with the length of a presentation. Someone even quoted a ratio of 2 minutes of presentation for every visual. It doesn't work that way. Two minutes is too long to look at the same image. It's the number of ideas being presented and the complexity of the ideas that dictate length of presentation. Keep in mind that it takes the same amount of time to present one idea on each of five visuals as it does to present five ideas on one visual.

6. Once you're convinced that the number and sequence of visuals is best, return to each visual and at the bottom of the page, **indicate the oral transition**—what you'll say that leads you from one visual to the next.

This is what your storyboard might look like when you're finished. Take a look.

1

INTRODUCTION (Oral)

PURPOSE — Our purpose today is to recommend that J.J. Ltd. explore the opportunities for growth offered by the attractive U.S. market

IMPORTANCE — This is most timely since growth at home is limited by intensifying competition and government regulation.

PREVIEW — In our presentation, we will review the reasons why the U.S. presents attractive opportunities for J.J. Ltd., and then outline the next steps required to identify and capitalize on them.

TRANSITION — Now, let us turn our attention to our reason for saying that the U.S. market is an attractive growth opportunity

2

U.S. IS AN ATTRACTIVE GROWTH OPPORTUNITY

A. U.S. IS THE WORLD'S LEADING ECONOMY

B. U.S. BANKING RETURNS ARE MOST ATTRACTIVE

C. BARRIERS TO ENTRY CAN BE OVERCOME

SO WHAT

We believe the U.S. market holds attractive opportunities for J.J Ltd for three reasons: the U.S. is the world's leading economy; it offers attractive returns; and the barriers to entry can be overcome.

TRANSITION

Let us study each in more depth. First, the U.S. is the world's leading economy. Here we look at three important measures of performance: GDP, foreign trade, and foreign direct investment.

3

U.S.: LARGEST SHARE OF WORLD GDP

United States 23%

Others 56

8 U.S.S.R.

7 Japan

6 Germany

SO WHAT

In term of gross domestic product, we find a better than 20% share of the world's GDP. This is more than the sum of the next three countries.

TRANSITION

Not only does the U.S. have the largest share of the world's economy, it has more foreign trade than any other country

4

U.S.: MOST FOREIGN TRADE

	Imports	Exports	Billions
United States			$207
Germany			158
Japan			118
France			99
U.K.			93
Canada			69
Netherlands			67

SO WHAT

Combining imports and exports, the U.S. generated over $200 billion in foreign trade last year – 30% more than Germany, the next largest foreign trader.

TRANSITION

In addition, the U.S. controls considerable foreign direct investment, and that investment is projected to increase significantly.

SO WHAT

Today the U.S. controls $65 billion of foreign direct investment. In 5 years, we project increase of 70% to over $100 billion. As you see, this is substantially greater than any other country.

5

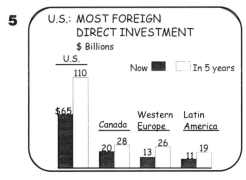

U.S.: MOST FOREIGN DIRECT INVESTMENT

$ Billions

U.S. 110

Now ■ ☐ In 5 years

$65

Canada 20 28

Western Europe 13 26

Latin America 11 19

TRANSITION

Projector off – These three findings – that the U.S. has the world's largest GDP; that it has more foreign trade; and that it controls considerable foreign direct investment – support our conclusion that the U.S. has the world's leading economy.

6

MORE OF SAME

7

U.S. IS AN ATTRACTIVE
GROWTH OPPORTUNITY

A. U.S. IS THE WORLD'S
LEADING ECONOMY

B. U.S. BANKING RETURNS
ARE MOST ATTRACTIVE

C. BARRIERS TO ENTRY
CAN BE OVERCOME

SO WHAT
In addition to
being the world's
leading economy,
the U.S. also
offers attractive
banking returns

TRANSITION
Here, we compare U.S. banking returns with those in other
countries, etc.

8

ENDING (Oral)

SUMMARY To summarize, the U.S. market appears to be an
attractive growth opportunity because of size,
returns, and relative ease of entry.

RECOMMENDATION Therefore, we recommend that J.J Ltd. proceed with
efforts to identify specific opportunities within this
market and to capitalize on them. To do so, we propose
the following program:

ACTION PROGRAM Gantt chart

NEXT STEPS 1. Identify specific segments that take advantage
of J.J. Ltd.'s strengths

2. Determine resources required

3. Etc.

DELIVER THE PRESENTATION

Confidence, conviction, and enthusiasm are the qualities that audiences look for when you stand up to deliver the presentation. They are the mark of a professional speaker. They are what enables the audience to concentrate on your message and participate with you as you move through the story and the visuals. More about each.

CONFIDENCE
conviction
enthusiasm

For the past 30-plus years, I've observed that the philosophy of life of most businesspeople has been *No pain, no gain*. Mine, on the other hand, has been *No strain, no pain*. Let me explain.

Like Woody Allen, I failed *milk* in kindergarten. As a result of the pain that came with that failure, I never enrolled in a course that I stood a chance of failing. (How else can I explain my proficiency at playing tennis, riding my bicycle, designing chess sets,[3] and drawing charts?) Similarly, I avoid the pain of being criticized; I prefer to hear about what I do well and to learn from that rather than to overcome the pain of discovering what I do poorly and then correcting it. When it comes to business presentations, I have learned more by studying the performance of good presenters, those who seem to deliver presentations effortlessly—that is, without pain.

Study good presenters and you'll notice that what makes them stand out from the crowd can be summarized in one word: *confidence*. They are confident that they'll be able to respond to any situation that might come up during their presentation. Think about it and you'll find that their confidence comes from knowing every aspect of their presentation.

---

[3]Take a look at my website *www.zelazny.com*.

THE MARK OF CONFIDENCE Because meeting the objective is the ultimate measure of success for any presentation, let me work backward through the process.

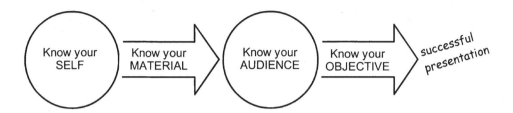

Good presenters have a clear sense of the *objective* of their presentation: They know why they're giving the presentation; they know what to expect as a result of the talk; they have confidence that the audience will make things happen so the goal they have set for the presentation is met.

Second, they have done their homework. They have learned everything they need to know about the members of the audience before the presentation. They really know their *audience:* They know whom they're talking to; they can read a question in the eyes of an individual before he raises his hand. It's more than knowing their audience; it's knowing the i.n.d.i.v.i.d.u.a.l.s in their audience.

Third, they're in touch with their *material,* so much so that they're not afraid to change the sequence of the story if a question leads them onto a side path. They seem ready to overcome doubt with supporting facts at all times.

Last, they appear comfortable with *themselves,* with their bodies, with their gestures, with their voices, with the equipment, with the visuals, with humor, with questions, and with their sense of being. They're not afraid to admit they don't have an answer to a question when they don't have one. They even make goofs look and sound natural.

Let's be clear: If you're not confident about *your* presentation, don't expect your audience to be.

Confidence
CONVICTION
enthusiasm

I was discussing the issue of speaking with conviction at one of the business schools. I talked about believing in what you're saying, about realizing that if you don't believe in what you're talking about, you can't expect your audience to be convinced either.

The student asked: "But what if your manager *orders* you to give the presentation, and you don't believe in the recommendation?"

Now I realize that my answer was not what he wanted to hear. For that matter, many in the audience would have argued that it was idealistic. Perhaps, but stay with me for a few moments.

I answered: "Don't do it." I went on to explain that if you don't believe in what you're presenting, the audience will sense it and they'll question the recommendations. It's better to have a discussion with your manager and express your feelings. It's better to find a colleague who does believe and who'll deliver the message convincingly. If all that fails, it's better to insist that you won't do it. Here's why.

If I'm your boss and you don't let me know that you disagree, you're not supporting me, because I'll see that lack of conviction while you're giving your presentation. You're not supporting yourself either, because there's a very good chance that I'll be upset with your performance.

In short, if you're not convinced of the soundness of your recommendations, if you don't feel that you would follow your own advice, don't expect your audience to either.

Confidence
conviction
ENTHUSIASM

I can promise you that you will seldom *bore* your audience into accepting your recommendations. When delivering any presentation, you get what you give: Give your audience boredom in the way you speak, and you're going to get boredom from them; give them enthusiasm, and you'll get enthusiasm back.

I can think of only one occasion when I, nonetheless, gave my full attention to a speaker who presented with little enthusiasm or energy. He spoke in a very low voice, with hardly any inflections, but I remember quietly sitting on the edge of my chair, and leaning forward, along with the rest of the audience, to make sure I would not miss out on any of his ideas. Why? He was speaking on a subject that was of the utmost importance to me, and he was widely known and respected for his intelligence and wisdom.

For the rest of us who may not have established our credentials yet, I would recommend speaking with energy and enthusiasm.

CONFIDENCE, CONVICTION, ENTHUSIASM It's the three working together that establishes your professional image in front of your audiences. That's what this chapter is all about. It contains pointers on *rehearsing, setting up the facilities and equipment, applying delivery skills, working with your visual aids, handling questions, using humor, and respecting the value of silence.*

REHEARSE:
THE SEARCH FOR
IMPERFECTION

Nowhere does the little voice in the back of my head scream as loud as when I anticipate standing up in front of an audience to deliver a presentation. Here's a sample of what I hear:

> I can't show I'm nervous.
>
> They won't like me.
>
> They'll embarrass me.
>
> They'll look for what I don't know.
>
> They'll look for something to disagree with.
>
> They'll see me sweat.
>
> I'll have to impress them with how much work I did.
>
> I'll have to justify the time I put into preparing.
>
> I'll have to justify the fees.

I'll leave spaces for you to fill in what *your* voice says
to you:

◆

◆

◆

◆

What is it about the prospect of standing up in front of
an audience that causes so much fear? Are we afraid of
making a mistake, of looking bad, of losing face or, to
put it euphemistically, of making an ass of ourselves?
Krishnamurti, the Indian guru, surfaces the concern best
when he asks, "When our feelings get hurt, what gets
hurt?"

The irony is that nothing physical hurts when our feelings
get hurt; it isn't like having a tooth pulled. Yet, there's so
much discomfort that, at times, we would rather have the
tooth pulled. Certainly, this fear has caused many a bad
moment for many of us. My moment of moments came
early in my career.

There I was, giving a training presentation to a small audience. There **HE** was, sitting to my right, taking up a dispro-
portionate amount of psychological space. About 15
minutes into the presentation, I heard his throaty, raspy
voice, **"There's a typo on that chart."** I felt the terror: He
found *my* mistake on *my* visual during *my* presentation.
Not just any he, but **HE,** the most feared if only because of
his sharp mind. For a few moments I felt my body temperature rise and I wanted to hide.

He was right; the vertical scale on the chart read, 0, 2, 4, 6,
8, 10, *13, 15.* What could I do? What could I say? Would
that I had had the quickness of mind to say what one of the
participants said: "Gene wanted to see if you were paying
attention, Darth."

Probably, the biggest change is that I'm no longer afraid to be wrong; I'm no longer afraid to admit that I've made a mistake. We learn from making mistakes; they tell us what to do next.

I've observed that admitting I made a mistake—and *thanking* the observer for pointing it out to me—makes the person feel good. It gives that person the feeling that she or he is contributing to the success of the presentation, supporting me so that I can do something about the error that she or he pointed out.

In other words, I've learned that it's all right to be human. I notice speakers feel they have to be perfect when they stand in front of an audience. They build into their mind's eye the image of a professional speaker. WOW! What an image! The speaker is never at a loss for words; the speaker speaks only in the most fluid, grammatically correct sentences; the speaker always has a brilliant answer for every question; and so it goes.

The truth is that no such speaker exists. As a matter of fact, the more perfect we try to be in front of an audience, the less human we seem, because to be human *is* to be imperfect. Let's face it, basketball would be dull if perfect humans played the game; it's the human failings, the errors, that make the game as exciting as it is.

Why is it so hard to get to the point where we can be ourselves, natural, comfortable, un-self-conscious about what we're doing with our bodies, our gestures, our voices? Chances are it's because we're afraid that people won't like the way we are. Worse, that *we* won't like the way we are. And, so we work to become someone we're not—to become our image of a perfect presenter. Only after a long struggle do we learn that we'll never be comfortable being someone we're not. The only person we can be comfortable with is ourselves, warts and all.

The truth is that we, *you and I, are going to make mistakes.* We *are* going to say the wrong thing at the wrong time; we *are* going to give a wrong answer; we *are* going to show the wrong visual; we *are* going to have a typo in the most important visual; and what we're going to realize is that *the members of the audience don't care.* If they do, they forget about it a great deal faster than we do. So, we may as well go with the flow, acknowledge that we're human, make our mistake, and move on.

All this is not to say that we shouldn't do all we can to make a presentation go well. That's where rehearsals come in, where we can practice the things we should think about to make it likely that we will deliver a professional presentation.

When you think about the stature of the audience, the importance of meeting the objective, the time and money invested in the preparation—it simply doesn't make sense to muff the presentation by not rehearsing, least of all for reasons such as, "I don't have time," or, "I don't want to lose my spontaneity." Let's not overrate spontaneity: The echoes of unfortunate ad-libs continue to rattle the walls of many conference rooms. Let's think it through before the presentation; during is too late.

The first rehearsal is by yourself, standing up in a room that simulates the one you'll be presenting in. The purpose here is to get comfortable with the material, to think through what you're going to say about each visual, to jot down the transitions, to check the timing of the presentation. A good idea is to use a tape recorder so you can hear yourself and decide whether the tone is appropriate, or whether any material should be reworded.

The second rehearsal is in front of three or four colleagues, including some who are familiar with the situation and others who aren't, toward the goal of building confidence. Ask each to concentrate on a different aspect of the presentation: One can look at the consistency of content, analyses, and structure; another can look for clarity and typos; a third can concentrate on delivery skills; a fourth should look at the presentation from the prospective decision maker's point of view. Also, this is the time to anticipate all the questions that may come up, including the three toughest questions from members of the audience with the highest stake—and to formulate clear, concise answers for them.

This can also be a good time to videotape the rehearsal so you can see yourself from the audience's point of view. A good idea here is to look at the video in two ways: (1) turning off the picture and concentrating on what you're saying and how you're saying it (choice of words, tone, enunciation, pronunciation, pace, and so on); (2) turning off the sound and focusing on your stance, gestures, facial expressions, working with the visuals, and so on.

When do you know that you've had enough rehearsal? When you feel you can approach the presentation tomorrow with the confidence, conviction, and enthusiasm that the situation deserves.

A NOTE TO REHEARSERS

When I ask you to sit through my rehearsal, I beg you to remember that the presentation is tomorrow, and this is not the time to undermine my confidence; I'm short of emotional Band-Aids. I ask you to:

> **Be sensitive.** Give me a chance to warm up before puncturing my confidence with negative observations; tell me the good about what I'm doing before the bad; use *I* statements, such as "I didn't understand the point of the chart," or "I'd be confused if I were a member of the audience," instead of *"You aren't* gonna use *that* chart, are *you?"* Ouch!

> **Be constructive.** Don't state a problem without a suggested solution. Help me know what to do to resolve the problems you've identified.

Be objective. I'm sorry that you don't like the color I used for the background of my visuals. However, because it won't make any difference to the message or to the audience, let it be. Please reserve your comments for things I do or say or show that will get in the way of comprehension.

Be realistic. Suggesting changes is like eating potato chips—it's practically impossible to stop at one. There's always room for improvement, but the presentation is tomorrow, and I'd like to get some sleep before getting to the presentation site, so please, help me concentrate on only those changes we can do something about.

Thank you. It's now time to move on to the presentation site and see what must be done to prepare the facilities and the equipment.

SET UP THE FACILITIES AND THE EQUIPMENT

Based on my own hard experience when it comes to setting up the facilities, my advice is for you to arrive at the presentation site at least 40 minutes early and to take total responsibility. This is truly an area where if anything can go wrong, it will, and that will undermine the confidence you've worked to develop so far. This is even more true as the media become more sophisticated. Here's the tip of the iceberg for all that can go wrong and how I've learned to handle the situations.

THE FACILITIES ARE DOING IT TO YOU

PROBLEM The light panel requires a rocket scientist to operate . . . if you can find it in the first place. What about temperature controls? What about the window shades?

I make sure to know where the light panel is and I test the switches so that I can decide which lights should be on, which should be off, and whether any need to be dimmed. I make sure that the lights over the screen are turned off.

I ask about what it takes, or whom to call, to turn the temperature up or down if it becomes necessary to make the room comfortable.

I play with the window shades, checking to see which can be raised to make sure the outside sunlight doesn't wash out the image on the screen, or distract the audience from paying attention to what's happening in the room.

PROBLEM I've noticed that the tables are often arranged with little thought.

I've opened the sides of a U-shaped table arrangement so that it looks more like a V; that arrangement opens up the space at the front of the room.

I've arranged the tables on either side of the center aisle so that they are angled in a fish-bone arrangement.

I've made sure that the center aisle is wide so no one's head will get in the way of the projected image.

I've moved unneeded chairs out of the way so they don't distract.

PROBLEM The microphone is usually fixed on the lectern, limiting your ability to move when you need, say, to go to the screen to point to an important part of a chart.

I request a lavaliere, or a lapel, or a wireless microphone so that I am not a prisoner of the lectern. Come to think of it, I seldom use a lectern; it's always too high for me and it creates a physical and psychological barrier between me and the audience. When I must use a lectern for my notes, I make sure to begin at the side of the lectern so the audience is aware of the total me rather than just the top of my bald head. (*An important note of caution if you're using a wireless microphone: Make sure to turn it off when not addressing the audience . . . AND when you go to the bathroom.*)

THE PROJECTOR IS DOING IT TO YOU

PROBLEM I've noticed that the overhead projector is invariably set up on the conference table so that members of the audience sitting behind it need to do gymnastics to see what's on the screen. Also, the projector becomes the focal point of the presentation, rather than the speaker.

I've hijacked a cocktail table out of a CEO's office, or from a reception area; I've used a piano stool; I've turned a trash can upside down; I've used the seat of a chair; anything 18 inches high to get the projector below the line of sight of those sitting behind it.

PROBLEM I've noticed that no two projectors are alike. No two projectors have the same on-off switch in the same place. No two projectors project with the same level of brightness. No two laptops use the same software. No two LCD projectors have the same wiring. No two remote controls are set up the same.

I make sure to test all the switches on the projector, all the connections on the laptop, all the remote control features. I make sure the wires are out of the way, or, at the very least, covered with tape.

PROBLEM I promise you that, during the most important presentation of your life, to the most important audience you've ever faced, at the most crucial moment, the bulb is going to blow.

So? How many of us think to bring a spare bulb? Come to think of it, it doesn't matter. How many of us know how to change the spare bulb? Oh, sure, all projectors have built-in spare bulbs . . . Wrong!

I check to make sure that the projector does have a built-in spare bulb. I find out where the switch is that changes the bulb and whether the second bulb is working. I incur the extra cost of having a second projector in the room, and I test it to make sure that it works. It's a small price to pay given the importance of the members of my audience.

PROBLEM I notice that no projector ever gets cleaned once it's been purchased.

I make sure to wipe the mirrors, the lenses, the stage of the projectors with a damp cloth.

THE SCREEN IS DOING IT TO YOU

PROBLEM We usually settle for whatever screen is in the room without considering options. As it happens, screens come in two sizes: too small or too small; with four types of surfaces: matte, lenticular, beaded, or translucent.

I generally request an 8-foot × 6-foot screen for presentations to groups of up to 50 people—and as large as will fit the room for larger audiences. Unless it's rear-projection, I insist on a matte screen. It's true that lenticular and beaded screens provide brighter reflection, but only for those members of the audience sitting directly in front of the screen. The image becomes progressively grayer toward the sides of the room. On a matte screen, the image projects with the same intensity no matter where you sit.

I've projected on the wide side of the room instead of on the narrow so that the audience would feel less confined.

I've placed the screen in the corner of the room; it was the only way to avoid the columns that were blocking the view of the screen.

I tilt the screen forward at the top to avoid the distortion of the image on the screen (called *keystone*) that results from having the projector sitting on a low table.

At all times, I raise the screen as close to the ceiling as possible to make it easier for members of the audience to look over one another's heads.

Closing message: **Don't delegate.**

Get into the room early.

Refuse to be at the mercy of inanimate objects.

Make the changes yourself.

APPLY DELIVERY SKILLS

You're ready to deliver the presentation. What does it take to make a good and lasting impression? I just received an e-mail from my daughter Donna, who closed with this apt thought for the answer: *"Dance as if nobody's watching."* Very often, we're at our best when we're not concerned about what people think of us. After all, we've planned carefully and rehearsed thoroughly. Here are some pointers that will help you be at ease before your audience.

BREATHE BREATHE B R E A T H E

Concentrating on breathing is probably the finest advice I can offer to overcome the nervous tension that comes with presenting in front of an audience. As you begin the presentation, take a moment to absorb what's going on in the room and take a couple of deep breaths. Take a breath before answering questions. Take a breath whenever you feel the need to relax.

ESTABLISH EYE CONTACT

Establishing eye contact at the beginning and throughout the presentation ranks among the most important delivery skills to master if you're to be successful in front of audiences. It distinguishes *a presentation at* from *a communication with* your audience.

Eye contact is a psychological handshake; it makes the members of the audience feel engaged, as if you're having a personal conversation with each of them. And, when I say "eye contact," I mean "**eye contact.**" I don't mean the stare that I see so often, where the speaker's eyes go out into the room about 12 inches before he or she realizes that it's dangerous to look farther.

When speaking to a large group, I suggest you pick out an individual in each quadrant of the audience—preferably someone who's smiling rather than one who's frowning or yawning—and establish eye contact with each one in turn. Because the distance between you and the individual is far, those seated around the one you're looking at feel included in the eye contact.

TALK NATURALLY

Many of us write out what we're going to say. However, we often fail to realize that we express ourselves differently in writing than we do when speaking. If we were reading from a written script, here's how we would sound ordering breakfast from a waiter at a diner: "Good morning, Sir. The purpose of my presence here this morning is to order breakfast. I will require the following items: (a) eggs, (b) toast, (c) coffee. . . ." You get the idea.

Let's be natural and speak the way we normally speak—contractions, idioms, and all. If you are going to write your notes or script beforehand, make sure you write the way you speak.

By the way, it's okay to refer to notes to be sure you don't forget important material. However, it's not okay to be so dependent on the notes that you appear to be talking to the notes rather than to the audience. The best thing to do is stay quiet while looking at your notes and then look up at the audience once you know what to say.

When working with a script, keep in mind that it usually takes about a minute and 20 seconds to talk through a double-spaced page of 12-point type. Type the script in a type size that will make the words easily legible for you when looking down at the lectern. Highlight the words you want to emphasize (*with underlines or bold type*) and indicate where you need to pause. One way to do this is to use a single slash for short pauses and double slashes for longer pauses. Indicate where the visual should be changed (*I use an asterisk for this*). Here's an example of such a marked-up script.

Let's take a look at the growth of commercial Web sites. There are approximately* **one million** today, up from* almost none 10 years ago. Their numbers will increase to* around **four million** next year.

In addition, the number of online households is **increasing dramatically.** In the United States, household connections rose* from 900,000 to* **over 20 million** today, for a compound annual growth rate of 43 percent. And that level of penetration is mirrored in* the United Kingdom and Japan, as well as other countries around the world.

We also expect that the amount of business to be conducted on the Internet will rise just as dramatically, going from* a little over $3 billion last year to something* near **$100 billion** by next year.

USE FULL VOCAL RANGE

I was riding my bicycle past a couple of youngsters when I heard one ask his friend, "How far can *you* talk? Me, I can talk to the end of the house." He proceeded to demonstrate by screaming at the top of his voice:

HELLOOOOOOOO HOOOOOOOUUUUSSSEEE!"

Now I'm not advocating screaming during presentations, but I am saying that you should use your full vocal range. Your voice should be a bit louder to emphasize the important points you're making and a bit softer to de-emphasize those that are less important. However, make sure that you always reach the people sitting in the back of the room, so they feel they're a part of the audience at all times. Addressing casual comments or quips only to the first row alienates the rest of the audience.

STAND WITH WEIGHT ON BOTH FEET, HANDS WAIST-HIGH

So many speakers seem unsure of what to do with their body and hands. I believe the heading says it all. If you stand with your weight evenly balanced on both feet, you guard against rocking from side to side or back and forth. If you bend your elbows and keep your hands in front of you about waist-high, you're likely to gesture naturally to reinforce what you're saying.

If you want to see yourself at your best, watch yourself on video describing your all-time-favorite vacation journey.

STAND BESIDE THE SCREEN

No matter what projection equipment you use, where to stand is an issue. Standing at the lectern throughout the presentation makes you less important than the visuals on the screen. Standing between the screen and the audience blocks the audience's view of the screen. Standing at the side of the room blocks a part of the audience. It also tempts you to divide your attention between the screen and the audience.

I suggest you stand beside the screen, turning your body at a 30-degree angle to the screen so you maintain eye contact with your audience. Then point with your nearest hand to the elements of the visual on the screen that you want the audience to focus on. The act of pointing makes it clear to the audience what they should look at and, and it's a big AND, it gives you something constructive to do with your body, which relaxes you.

Yes, but! What about the light that shines across your face and your body when you're reaching for something on the screen? Let it shine for the few seconds it takes you to point. Then step back out of the light as you explain the significance of the visual element you were pointing to.

There are times when you have no choice but to stand behind a lectern—for example, when you need to refer to a prepared script. However, remember that the lectern creates a physical and psychological barrier between you and your audience. Therefore, if you can avoid one, do so.

When you can't, at the very least, stand alongside the lectern during your introduction and during the ending of your presentation, with the room lights on. Move behind the lectern only as you begin to show your visuals, at which time the audience is no longer looking at you but at the image on the screen.

As I said earlier, to give yourself freedom of movement, request a lavaliere, or a lapel, or a wireless microphone instead of the microphone attached to the lectern.

DON'T USE A POINTER UNLESS NECESSARY

You have enough things in your hands without introducing something else to add to your nervousness. You have notes, and the remote controls, and the microphone cord, and your pen and . . . Enough.

I've noticed, as you probably have, that for many speakers, the pointer becomes a weapon. They use it to fence with members of the audience, or to slam the poor defenseless screen, or to smack the unsuspecting table. Worst of all, if it's collapsible, they constantly open and close it, which makes it distracting.

Better to let your body do what it's designed to do. Use your arm and your hand to point directly on the screen.

Yes, but! What if I can't reach what I want to point to? If you must, use a pointer. However, use it only for what it is meant to do: to point when you can't reach. Otherwise, put it down. Also, avoid those battery-operated pointers with the laser-light beam. To use those effectively, you need the accuracy of a basketball player trying to sink a hoop from midcourt. Besides, the movement of the light becomes a distraction.

Of course, for onscreen presentations, you can use the mouse to aim the pointer that comes with the software. Even then, minimize the distance the pointer needs to travel onscreen. The wavering can be distracting.

ADAPT FOR VIDEOCONFERENCES

While on the subject of making the most of delivery skills and visual aids, we should take a few moments to address the implications of presenting during videoconferences.

For the most part, the same recommendations apply, but with a few subtle distinctions given the time lag—the momentary delay that the signals take to reach the viewing audience.

1. There's a good chance that you'll be sitting instead of standing. Sit comfortably with your back straight, your feet flat on the ground, and your arms above the conference table.

2. Keep eye contact with the camera to give the audience members on the other side of the camera the feeling that you're speaking to them individually.

3. Continue to gesture comfortably.

4. Hold humor to a minimum. Humor works best when the punch line is practically instantaneous with the laughter of the audience. Given the current level of videoconference technology, the audience is still listening to the end of the joke as you and your colleagues on this side of the video are already laughing.

5. To narrow the psychological distance, learn the names of the members of the viewing audience and refer to them by name as you move through your presentation.

*   *   *

To further develop your delivery skills, it's a good idea to work with a professional who can make sensitive and constructive suggestions about how to present yourself in front of audiences. If possible, use video so you can see yourself from the audience's point of view.

WORK WITH YOUR VISUAL AIDS

We've just talked about how to talk and stand while giving a presentation. That's a lot to master, but the art of delivering a presentation doesn't end there. You also need to get comfortable with your visual aids as soon as you can so that using them becomes second nature. Here are my presentation secrets for how to work with your visuals.

Transition BEFORE changing visuals

Repeat after me: "Transition **BEFORE** changing visuals."
Again: "Transition **BEFORE** changing visuals."
Again: "Transition **BEFORE** changing visuals."

When showing visuals, whether as a handout or as 35-mm slides, overhead transparencies, onscreen, or whatever, give your audience the transition to what you're about to show on the next visual **BEFORE** you change the visual.

Most speakers show the visual before making the transition to the visual. When this happens, the audience doesn't know whether to read what's on the visual—which has not yet been addressed—or to listen to what the speaker is saying. The audience may also get the impression that the speaker needs to see the screen to know what to say. Unfortunately, when the speaker uses the visual as a cue card, he or she spends more time talking to the visual than to the audience. Can you blame the audience, then, for thinking that the speaker wasn't interested enough to prepare properly?

To be effective, the spoken words and the visual must work together; what we hear must reinforce what we see, and what we see must support what we hear. The transition links what we have just seen on the current visual to what we are about to see on the next.

Here's the four-step process for making effective transitions:

1. Continue eye contact with the audience as you finish discussing the previous slide.

> "As we've just seen, the United States holds tremendous potential for J.J. Ltd."

2. Hold the eye contact as you make the transition to the next slide.

> "But will J.J. be able to enter the U.S. market? In fact, there are no insurmountable barriers to entry."

3. Be quiet as you replace the old visual with the new one.

4. Make eye contact once more as you begin to tell the story of the new visual.

> "Here are the barriers you're familiar with, and the recommendations for overcoming them."

When you talk, TALK
When you change visuals, CHANGE VISUALS

Step 3 needs emphasis. Talking to the audience while changing visuals creates confusion. You're trying to juggle too many different tasks. More often than not, you need to break eye contact with the audience to watch what you're doing, so you end up talking to the visual or to the projector and forgetting that there's an audience out there.

It works better to say what you have to say with your eyes on your audience all the way to the end of your sentence. Then be quiet while changing visuals. That way, you concentrate fully on each task.

Don't be afraid of the silence while changing visuals; the audience appreciates it. Remember, you've given them the transition, so they're willing to take a few silent seconds to think about what's coming up.

LEAD THE AUDIENCE THROUGH EACH VISUAL

Once the visual is displayed:

1. Explain the elements of the chart.

> "On the vertical scale at the left . . . On the horizontal scale at the bottom."

> "At the top of this matrix, we identify the six competitors. Down the side we list the four criteria."

2. Define any coding you've used.

> "Note the three colors. Yellow represents . . ."

> "The solid line indicates . . . while the dashed line represents . . ."

3. Point out what the visual is designed to show.

> "Note the trend that's moving up diagonally from the lower left to the upper right."

> "Contrast the steady pattern of your competitor with the fluctuations of your company."

4. State the "so what" of the visual.

"So, we need to motivate the salespeople to think about the more profitable accounts."

"As a result, the high-tech market is an attractive one to enter."

5. Transition to the next visual.

"We've seen the many favorable aspects of the high-tech market. Let's now explore the things we have to be wary of."

CHANGE YOUR OWN VISUALS

Given the details you have to think about as you deliver your presentation, you'd probably appreciate having someone else change the visuals for you. Sorry, but I insist that you do it yourself. No one else can know the precise moment when the visual should be changed to get a smooth transition. Besides, sometimes you change your mind about when a visual should be changed, either because you want to amplify a thought or because you want to cut a thought short. In these situations, you'd have to alert the person doing the switching, which distracts from the smooth flow of the presentation.

When you have no choice—for example, at a large industry conference where the equipment is controlled by audio-visual personnel—I recommend that you work with a script and give a copy to the person controlling your visuals. *(In the previous chapter, I showed an example of a marked-up script.)* All the more need for rehearsal.

PROJECT A BLANK SCREEN

When using overhead projectors or LCD projectors, it's a good idea to turn the projector off periodically. I don't mean to suggest that you should turn the projector off after each visual; that can become distracting. It's a good idea, however, to have no visual showing during lengthy transitions, during lengthy summaries, between one speaker and the next, or while answering a question that has nothing to do with the image on the screen. It's another way to have the eye contact with the members of your audience that is so important in business presentations. *(Keep in mind that turning the projector off won't work in a large auditorium when the lights have been turned off. For a darkened room, you need to design a constant parade of visuals, including those to be shown during lengthy transitions. One thing you can do is repeat the agenda visual with emphasis on the segment you're in the process of discussing.)*

I realize that I'm giving you lots to think about. I didn't say it was easy, but I promise that, with a bit of experience and rehearsing, these pointers will become so natural that you won't have to think about them during the presentation, allowing you the time to concentrate on the content.

GET USED TO ANSWERING QUESTIONS

For many speakers, the major source of nervousness about making a presentation is the fear of questions—worse, the fear of not having answers. We show these fears when we use any of these defensive tactics.

DELAYING We say, for example, "Ladies and Gentlemen, please hold all of your questions to the end."

Since we know we'll never get to the end, we don't have to handle the questions.

CONTROLLING When someone asks a question, we say, "I'll get to that later," or, "I'll get to that in a few minutes." Those are the words we use, but what we communicate is, "Please stop interrupting me; I'll address your question once I'm comfortable that I have an answer."

In effect, we're telling the audience that what we have to say is more important than what they need to hear to follow what we're talking about. *(Judy recalls an executive who walked out of the room after the put-off. He told the presenter that he would be in his office waiting for the call that would let him know when the presenter had reached "later.")*

AVOIDING We turn our backs to the audience and read what's on the screen. *(We're especially prone to do this when we haven't spent enough time rehearsing.)*

Without eye contact, we don't need to acknowledge any questions.

CHALLENGING We design our charts with as much detail as we can squeeze in, including footnotes, assumptions, caveats, sources, every word we're going to say.

This dares the audience to embarrass itself by asking a question that must have been covered in some illegible footnote.

HIDING We use 35-mm slides or LCD projectors and darken the room more than necessary.

We can't see anyone raising his or her hand with a question. Even if we do see them, we have a good reason to make believe we can't spot them in the dark.

OVERWHELMING We speak rapidly, without pause, making certain we are never at a loss for words.

The audience can't find space between our ideas to ask its questions.

Where do questions come from? How can we make them disappear? Well, we can't. Or at least, we shouldn't try. What we should do is change our attitude toward questions. We need to understand that *the audience is not the enemy.* Members of the audience do not intend to put us on the spot by asking the one and only question for which we have no answer. What they are trying to do is get the information they need to understand the presentation. Their intent is to move through the logic of our ideas and eventually, to agree with us.

The best course is to get comfortable with the process of handling questions:

1. Be patient and **L I S T E N** to the question.

Usually, as a question is asked, we hear the metronome in our mind: "Do I have an answer? Don't I have the answer? Do I have an answer? Don't I have the answer? Oh great, I have an answer!" And, because we feel so good about having an answer, we interrupt before the questioner has a chance to finish.

WAIT. . . Often, in the process of asking the question, the individual answers his or her own questions.

WAIT. . . There may be a clue to the answer in the way the question is phrased.

WAIT. . . Sometimes someone else answers the question and you don't have to handle it.

WAIT. . . At times, the first question is not the real question; it's laying the groundwork for the question that follows.

WAIT. . . If only because it's common courtesy to let the person finish talking before you respond.

2. After the question has been asked, pause to think about your answer.

Pause before giving the answer. Make the person feel that the question is so important that you need time to think about the answer.

3. You need *not* repeat the question.

Repeat the question if you're not sure that everyone in the room has heard it. Repeat the question if you're not sure you understood it properly. Repeat the question if you need to reword it to answer it. Otherwise, pause until you're confident of your answer.

4. Answer only the question that's been asked, no more and no less.

Avoid giving an answer that's so detailed that the audience hears this: "Not only do I have an answer for that question, I have answers for questions that you haven't asked yet." Don't lose sight of the objective of the presentation, or of the time constraints.

5. Give your answer to the whole audience, not only to the person who asked.

Assume everyone is equally interested in the answer. Instead of maintaining eye contact only with the questioner, move your eyes so the whole audience feels included.

6. Stay with the question until you know you've answered it fully.

Ask the questioner if you've answered the question to his or her satisfaction. That way, you can make sure you didn't misunderstand the question or give an answer that was off base.

I hear your questions:

"What if it's a dumb question?"

Write the following sentence on the electronic white board 100 times after class:

THERE IS NO SUCH THING AS A DUMB QUESTION. I emphasized that thought to give it the importance it deserves. I assure you that, to the person asking, it isn't a dumb question. Instead of judging the question, answer it patiently and respectfully. The rest of the audience will appreciate the respect you're showing and will feel safer asking questions.

"What if the question is irrelevant?"

Answer the question.

"What if the question is hostile?"

Don't be a party to the hostility, the sarcasm, the whatever. Answer the content of the question, not the spirit . . . without hostility or sarcasm. Be professional and concentrate on making sure that what you have to say is understood and accepted.

"What if the question comes from someone who isn't important?"

Answer the question.

"What if one person is dominating with a flood of questions?"

Answer the questions patiently and briefly. Break eye contact at the end of the question and make eye contact with someone else. When all else fails, restate the objective of the presentation, point out the time constraints, ask the individual to note the questions so you and he or she can get together at the end of the session, AND, whatever you do, make sure your tone doesn't suggest what you'd like the person to do with the questions.

"What if I don't have an answer?"

Say so. Give the person credit for surfacing something you had not thought of. Here are several options for handling the situation.

> If you're part of a team, turn to the team members for ideas.

> Turn the question to the rest of the audience for insights.

> Build the question into the next steps.

> Let the person know that you'll find an answer, and that you'll get back to him or her with an answer as soon as possible. And then, **keep your promise.**

After all is said and done, the best way to handle questions is to anticipate them. Make it a part of your preparation for the presentation to surface the three toughest questions you expect from the members of the audience, and to think about your answers before the presentation. Better yet, if you know you're going to be asked those questions, pre-empt them by introducing them yourself as part of the presentation.

And through it all, remember **THE AUDIENCE IS NOT THE ENEMY.**

TAKE HUMOR SERIOUSLY

I recall, in my earlier days, relying on several cartoons for the introduction to my presentation at the business schools. While the audience laughed and I felt good, after a while, I realized that the humor was a cover-up for my nervousness, a plea to the audience to *be kind.* In time, I came to realize that my audience wanted the serious content of my presentation and that I did not need the crutch. Today I still use humor, but in a much more constructive way. For instance, I've learned:

Humor is great when it helps to make a point. Unrelated jokes or funny stories do not make a presentation great. What does work is to be human, to share personal experiences. Let the audience know that you've lived through similar situations and here's how they turned out for you. Make the audience feel that you'd follow your own advice. Show how your experiences support the points you're making.

You can use humor the same way you would use an exhibit that demonstrates a message more quickly than words alone would. For example, remember the "Dear

Shirley" letter I used earlier in this book? That was a use of humor to demonstrate optional ways of structuring your story line.

Humor is great if the situation is appropriate. That pretty much speaks for itself. Let's face it: the time to use humor is not when the presentation is addressed to a company that has just lost a chunk of market share.

Humor is great when it's spontaneous. I recall receiving a question, "Should the presenter repeat the question that's been asked?" As I was thinking about what to answer, and without giving thought to what I was doing, I said softly, "Should . . . the . . . presenter . . . repeat . . . the question . . . that's been asked?"

The bigger laugh came when I answered "No. Not usually."

Humor is great if you're comfortable with it. Use it only if it feels natural.

A few words of caution about the use of humor:

Do not ever, ever, ever use humor to attack anyone in the audience. I've sat through presentations where the speaker's sarcasm and cynicism were so heavy that the audience wanted to hide under the table. I know that some speakers think it's macho to make someone in the audience the butt of humor. It doesn't work. The audience is very self-protective. Attack one member, and all others will avoid eye contact with the speaker for fear that the humor will be directed at them next.

Make sure the point comes across quickly and clearly. There's no room for ambiguity. Relate the humor to the point you're making in the presentation. *(By the way, when using cartoons, make certain that the caption is brief, and that it is big, bold, and legible to the people in the last row. Also, place the caption at the top, above the cartoon, where there is a greater likelihood that the audience will be able to read it.)*

Be flexible. If you didn't get the reaction you expected after the first joke or cartoon, reserve the option not to use any others.

Last, and perhaps most important: **If you have doubts or discomfort about using humor, don't use it.**

LISTEN TO THE SILENCE

In the chapter on handling questions, I spoke about being patient—about letting the whole question be heard before rushing with an answer. Similarly, throughout the presentation, it's a good idea to *listen to the silence*.

It's similar to what you do when you open up a bottle of fine wine. You let the wine breathe; you give it a few moments to adapt to room temperature before serving it. It's the same with your ideas. Surround each idea with parentheses of silence. Give each idea a chance to breathe, to be absorbed, to be understood, to be reflected upon, to be appreciated by the members of your audience.

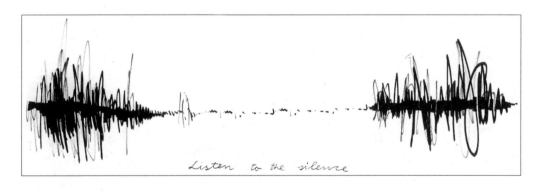

Listen to the silence

I asked Vera to design this card a few years ago when I came to appreciate the value of silence in communication. I remember walking into the CEO's office to argue a procedure that he disagreed with strongly. Believe me when I say that I had all my arguments lined up, rehearsed, and ready as I entered HIS office. I let loose the longest sentence without breathing ever recorded. At no time did I leave him so much as an opening to contradict, to comment. I gave him no chance to say anything lest he interrupt my flawless logic.

And so I went on until I ran out of air and my argument ran out of steam, if not out of logic. HE never said a word. I walked out, deflated. Since then, I've learned that silence can be one of our best friends for several reasons:

♦   It gives us a chance to think about what we're going to say, instead of rushing words before we've had a chance to put thoughts together.

♦   It separates the ideas so that instead of talking on and on for fear that someone is going to interrupt us with a question, we can express our first idea . . . let it sink in . . . move on to the second idea . . . let it sink in. That way, each idea is given the attention it deserves.

♦   It allows the audience to think about what we've said, rather than contending with an avalanche of ideas that come too quickly to be understood.

♦   It gives the audience a chance to contribute. After all, we don't learn anywhere near as much by talking all the time as we do by listening some of the time.

One of my colleagues called it *the courage to be quiet.* I like that. Study the great speakers, study the great comedians, and you'll note that a great deal of their success is due to their mastery of the art of *shutting up.*

CLOSING THOUGHTS

SO YOU'RE GOING TO GIVE A PRESENTATION

As I said in the beginning, learning to give a presentation is like learning to ride a bicycle. You won't get very far just by reading the manual. With bike riding, you must learn how to balance, pedal, steer, and stop before you can coast down a hill with confidence and a smile on your face. Similarly, you must learn how to design and deliver a successful presentation before you can walk to the front of a conference room with confidence and a smile on your face.

My hope is that my ideas and insights will make giving a presentation easier for you, even if it never becomes as enjoyable as a day on the bike trail.

For now, I suggest that you make a copy of the following checklist and refer to it each time you're designing a presentation to make sure you've followed the steps to a successful presentation.

SAY IT WITH PRESENTATIONS

1. DEFINE THE SITUATION

Specify your objective

- ◆ Why are you giving a presentation?
- ◆ What do you hope to accomplish?
- ◆ What do you want the audience to do or think as a result of the presentation?

Analyze your audience

- ◆ Who are the decision makers?
- ◆ How familiar with the subject are they?
- ◆ How interested in the subject are they?
- ◆ What do they stand to gain if they say Yes and what do they stand to lose?
- ◆ Why should they say No?

	◆ What are the three toughest questions you're going to get from the audience?
Define the scope	◆ Can you meet the objective in the allotted time?
Select the medium	◆ Handouts, easels, electronic boards for informal discussions, fact review sessions, interactive meetings.
	◆ Transparencies, onscreen/LCDs for semiformal, progress reviews.
	◆ Onscreen/LCDs, 35-mm slides, multimedia, videos for formal, final presentations.

2. DESIGN THE PRESENTATION

Determine the message	◆ How would you summarize the presentation if you had only 30 seconds?
Craft the story line	
INTRODUCTION	◆ Purpose.
	◆ Importance.
	◆ Preview.
BODY	◆ *To a receptive audience:* conclusions and recommendation up front.

	◆ *To an unreceptive audience:* conclusions at the end of each chapter or (if you must) at the end of the presentation.
ENDING	◆ Summary.
	◆ Recommendation(s).
	◆ Action program.
	◆ Next steps.
Build the storyboard	◆ Design the visuals.

WHAT Text, pictures, models

WHERE Maps, plans

WHO Organization charts, photographs

WHEN Calendars, Gantt charts

HOW Diagrams

HOW MUCH Tables, charts

WHY Text

◆ Sequence the visuals: Develop what you're going to say and a transition for each.

Produce the visuals and the supporting handouts.

3. DELIVER THE PRESENTATION

REHEARSE 1
- ◆ Get thoroughly familiar with story and visuals.
- ◆ Prepare notes.
- ◆ Practice with a tape recorder.

REHEARSE 2
- ◆ Practice with colleagues who are sensitive, constructive, objective, and realistic.
- ◆ Anticipate questions.
- ◆ See yourself on video.

Set up the facilities
- ◆ Get to the room 40 minutes early and take responsibility for setting up facilities and equipment.

Apply delivery skills
- ◆ Breathe, breathe, breathe.
- ◆ Establish eye contact.
- ◆ Talk naturally.
- ◆ Use full vocal range.
- ◆ Weight on both feet.
- ◆ Hands waist high.
- ◆ Stand beside screen.

Work with visual aids
- ◆ Establish transition before changing visuals.
- ◆ Reveal visual.

more . . .

	◆ Lead audience through each visual.
	◆ Remove visual.
Handle questions	◆ Establish eye contact.
	◆ Listen patiently.
	◆ Pause before answering.
	◆ Answer question, no less, no more.
	◆ Transition back to presentation.

MEASURE OF SUCCESS:

HAVE YOU MET YOUR OBJECTIVE?

From: *Say It with Presentations*, Gene Zelazny.
McGraw Hill, Copyright 2000

APPENDIX

SAY IT WITH LAP VISUALS

In this book, I've concentrated on presentations in which the speaker addresses a relatively large audience and the visuals are projected onto a screen. There are situations, however, when the speaker sits down at a conference table and addresses a small group, and each member has a copy of the visuals to review while the speaker is talking. Because this type of presentation (sometimes called "lap visuals") is growing in popularity, I'd like to take a few moments to describe it in more detail.

Basically, lap visual presentation packs are composed of a series of charts and text visuals. Sometimes the pages are simply stapled together and sometimes they are bound into a handout. They are used to prompt informal interaction with the group—a free-flowing exchange of ideas—so listening and responding to the audience members' comments is as important as—or more important than—presenting your point of view, which makes it very different from a stand-up presentation. This type of presentation is most appropriate for small meetings—ideally with not more than three or four people.

The primary purpose of lap visuals is to build consensus. You can use them to test your work to date, to check the accuracy of facts that you've researched, to identify sources for missing facts, to surface issues, to make sure your action programs will work. You can also use them to gain agreement on conclusions or acceptance of recommendations.

Because interactive meetings of this sort can easily digress from the main theme, it's important for you to keep the discussion moving toward its objective and to focus everyone's attention on the same idea. Here are tips on how to provide the necessary leadership—how to prepare the visual and how to present it.

PREPARING THE LAP VISUAL

Because the reason for using a lap visual is to generate interaction among the participants, you need to plan carefully despite its apparent informality. Just as you would with a stand-up presentation, before the meeting, establish what you want to accomplish and analyze the members of the audience. Think about each participant: How well informed will he or she be? What can you expect each to contribute? How is each likely to react? In the process, ask yourself if you really need the meeting—will the results justify the cost to prepare and the time to attend?

If the answer is "Yes," select the materials you'll need and structure them in the sequence that will best meet the needs of the participants and make it easy for you to reach your objective. Also, make sure to have backup exhibits in case you need them to further support the discussion. In designing the visuals, bear in mind that you want them to be the basis *for* discussion, not the basis *of* discussion. That is, you want the discussion to be about what each visual implies, not about how it's designed. To this end, distinguish what you're going to say from what you're going to show.

Charts should be simpler than those you would use in a written document. Use topic titles ("Sales Trends") if you want members of the audience to reach their own conclusions about the facts shown and to discuss them; use message titles ("Sales Are Seasonal") if you want to stress a point and have a discussion about its implications.

Keep text visuals to a minimum: Only use them to structure the presentation or a chapter and to reinforce important thought groupings, such as findings, conclusions, recommendations, next steps. And make them brief. Consider phrases rather than full sentences. For example:

> **Not:** We project that within 1 to 2 years, Company A and Company B will compete for the same sales territories, sales force, suppliers, and consumers, with potentially drastic consequences for the loser.

> **But:** Competition between Company A and B will intensify

Once the lap visual is produced, prepare yourself for the meeting. On each page of your copy, underline or circle words, numbers, and references to be emphasized, and write reference notes.

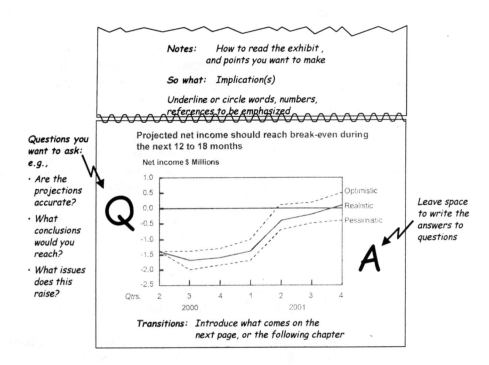

PRESENTING THE LAP VISUAL

Throughout the meeting, keep in mind that your role is to keep the discussion going. Therefore, you need to keep an open mind to the participants' points of view, avoid a right/wrong attitude, listen attentively, establish a constructive tone, and concentrate on talking with the participants, not at the visual.

INTRODUCTION

As you start the meeting, become part of the group by participating in the conversation and look for the appropriate moment to:

1. Gain agreement to the *purpose* of the meeting—what to expect as the outcome. Remember that the participants may have a different agenda from yours; give them time to be heard.

2. Establish the *importance* of the meeting to the participants and to the project that's being discussed.

3. Present a *preview* of what you'll cover during the meeting, how you propose to go through the material, and possibly what you expect each member to contribute.

It's almost always a good idea to handle this introduction orally—before you hand out the copies of the lap visuals. This approach focuses attention on the discussion, not the visuals, and establishes you as the discussion leader. Also, it keeps the participants from leafing through the document before you've established how best to go through it to make the most of the discussion.

BODY

Be patient. Remember that you've seen the material before, but the participants are unfamiliar with it. Focus their attention on what you want them to look at in their copy of the visuals. Then give them time to read and understand it. Also, remember that, unlike a stand-up presentation, you can't point to what you want them to look at; you need to give them oral clues about how best to study each visual.

1. Direct them to the specific page.

   "On page . . . On the next three pages . . ."

2. Explain the elements of the chart.

   "On the vertical scale at the left . . . On the horizontal scale at the bottom . . ."

   "At the top of the matrix, I've identified the six competitors. Down the side, I've listed the four criteria."

3. Define any coding you've used.

   "Note the three colors; the blue represents . . ."

   "As you see, the solid red trend line indicates . . . while the green line represents . . ."

4. Point out what the visual is designed to show.

   "Note the trend that's moving up diagonally from the lower left to the upper right."

   "Contrast the steady pattern of your competitor with the fluctuations of your company."

5. If appropriate to your objective, state the "so what" of the visual.

   "So, we need to motivate the sales people to think more about the profitable accounts."

   Or ask the group what they think the "so what" is.

   "Do you think this suggests a need for change in the sales incentives?"

6. Finish each page with a transition to what follows on the next page or in the next chapter.

At all times, be sure to raise the questions you need to ask and note the answers.

On occasion, you may want to hold up your copy of the visual and point to it so everyone sees to what you're referring.

For text visuals, either read them as they are written, or be quiet while the audience members read for themselves.

At times, you may want to place a pencil at the page, close the pack, look at the participants, and enter into a discussion with them.

Throughout the meeting, stay flexible and responsive to the discussion. Skip details of the visuals the participants have clearly accepted. Be prepared to change the sequence of points. Jump ahead or omit visuals in response to comments or questions.

ENDING

As I mentioned, the reason for using a lap visual is to generate interaction. The discussion may be longer than you expected. Allow sufficient time for closing remarks, even if it means deleting pages or segments of the presentation. In your closing comments, summarize what happened during the meeting and gain commitment to:

◆ **Areas of agreement.**

◆ **Unresolved questions.** Particularly concerns expressed by the audience members.

◆ **Next steps.** That is, the plan of action for resolving open questions, including names of individuals you would follow up with; sources of material you need to study further; and date, time, and place for subsequent meetings. Also, confirm the things the participants have agreed to do.

As with your introduction, it's best to handle the ending orally, although you may want to record the next steps that you've agreed to on a separate sheet of paper.

USING DELIVERY SKILLS

As with stand-up presentations, take advantage of your delivery skills to establish a tone of confidence, conviction, and enthusiasm.

◆   Sit up in your chair; plant your feet flat on the ground.

◆   Maintain eye contact with the individuals as much as possible.

◆   Use gestures to emphasize what you're saying.

◆   Speak naturally, and talk with the audience, not to the visual.

◆   Be responsive to the participants' body language. For example, when an individual is slouching in his or her chair, raise your energy level; when he or she is nodding impatiently, move on to new material.

In short, the lap visual is an interactive medium that is useful for building consensus. Your goal in meetings at which lap visuals are used is to get the audience members involved and encourage them to contribute to the solution of the problem under discussion. Your role is to provide leadership for the discussion to make sure that the objective of the meeting is achieved. The trick is to cover the essential points while remaining responsive to the flow of the discussion.

INDEX

ABOUT THE AUTHOR

Gene Zelazny is the Director of Visual Communications for McKinsey & Company.

Since joining the Firm in 1961, Gene's primary responsibility has been to provide creative advice and assistance to the professional staff in the design of visual presentations and written reports. This includes planning the communication strategy; structuring the story line; interpreting the data or concepts and recommending the best visual formats in terms of charts, diagrams, and so on; designing storyboards; and rehearsing the presenters. Also, he has designed and led communication training programs throughout the Firm.

On behalf of the Firm, Gene regularly presents his ideas on *Making the Most of Your Business Presentation* at business schools including Chicago, Columbia, Cornell, Darden, Harvard, Haas, Kellogg, Michigan, Sloan, Stanford, Tuck, UCLA, Wharton, Washington, in the United States, and INSEAD, LBS, and Oxford in Europe.

His book, *Say It with Charts,* is in its third edition in the United States and is available in French, German, Italian, Portuguese, and Spanish.

Otherwise, you'll find him on a tennis court or on a bicycle, designing chess sets and sponsoring children to do the same (check out his Web site at www.zelazny.com), writing essays for his friends, and always holding hands with Judy.